AUSTRALIA'S TIMELESS
GARDENS

Christmas and
Mother's Day 1999

All my love and hugs

Becky

xxxxxx

AUSTRALIA'S TIMELESS
GARDENS

Written by
Judith Baskin
with
Trisha Dixon

National Library of Australia
Canberra
1996

Published by the National Library of Australia
Canberra ACT 2600

Every reasonable endeavour has been made to contact relevant copyright holders. Where this has not proved possible, the copyright holders are invited to contact the publishers.

National Library of Australia Cataloguing-in-Publication entry

Baskin, Judith.
     Australia's timeless gardens.

     Includes index.
     ISBN 0 642 10668 1.

     1. Gardens—Australia—History. 2. Gardens—Australia—Pictorial works. 3. Historic gardens—Australia. 4. Historic gardens—Australia—Pictorial works. 5. Gardens—Australia—Design—History. 6. Gardens—Australia—Design—Pictorial works. I. Dixon, Trisha, 1953– . II. National Library of Australia. III. Title.

712.60994

Designer: Andrew Rankine
Editor: Robyn Carter
Printed by Goanna Print, Canberra

Cover: Augustus Earle, 1793–1838
Government House and Part of the Town of Sidney [sic] *N.S. Wales,* 1828
watercolour; 18.1 x 31.1 cm
Rex Nan Kivell Collection; Pictorial Collection

Inset: One of the most ancient of plants, the King protea (*Protea cynaroides*) dates back 300 million years to the super continent of Gondwana before it broke up to form Australia, Africa, South America, New Zealand and New Guinea
Photograph by Trisha Dixon

C O N T E N T S

Acknowledgements vi

Introduction vii

Note on Plant Names viii

Chapter 1 The First Garden 1

Chapter 2 The Garden Grows 15

Chapter 3 Through the Artist's Eye 25

Chapter 4 Back to Basics 39

Chapter 5 The Garden Designer 49

Chapter 6 An Evolution 67

Select Bibliography 82

Glossary 84

Index 85

ACKNOWLEDGEMENTS

Many people have been of great assistance to us in producing *Australia's Timeless Gardens*. In particular, we would like to thank Kate Fortune, formerly of the National Library of Australia. Her coordinating role and support were much appreciated. Also, we would like to thank the staff of the Pictorial section whose love of the collection is reflected in their helpful and interested attitude.

Thanks also to Ralph Neale and *Landscape Australia* magazine for permission to reproduce photographs; Victor Crittenden for his support, both through his writings and his advice; Stuart Read for being a careful custodian of botanical names; and Robyn Carter and Andrew Rankine for producing a lovely book.

Judith Baskin and Trisha Dixon
Canberra

L ooking at other people's gardens is an Australian national pastime. For many, it takes the form of a stroll through the neighbourhood on a Sunday afternoon. For others, it is a more serious, organised passion. Horticultural societies, garden clubs, the Australian Garden History Society, Australia's Open Garden Scheme, charities and municipalities all conduct garden visits, like those of the embassy gardens in the national capital. The aim of this book is to offer a very different garden tour, one that provides a picture of Australia's private gardens as they have developed over more than 200 years.

It draws on images selected from the Pictorial Collection of the National Library of Australia—a collection rich in images from private and public gardens, botanical gardens, nurseries, reserves and national parks. Our concentration is on the private gardens, but our story begins with a public one: the garden of the first Government House in Sydney. From there, we follow the development of private gardens from white settlement to the present day. The sketches, paintings, engravings and photographs chosen reflect the rich and varied history of gardens in Australia, their evolution and their timelessness.

In general, common names of plants are followed by their botanical names in brackets, for example Swan River cypress (*Actinostrobus pyramidalis*). In some instances, where the plants are well known and it would seem pedantic to insert the botanical names, the common names only are used, for example eucalypts, roses, iris, wattle. However, if a particular species is referred to, its common name is given followed by the botanical name, for example black wattle (*Acacia mearnsii*) or black wattle (*Calliccma serratifolia*), to avoid confusion between plants. For many Australian plants there is no generally accepted common name and the botanical name of the genus is used. In such cases the botanical name only is given, for example *Hakea* spp. All botanical names are in italics. In the index botanical names are given in full with a reference from the common name.

CHAPTER 1
The First Garden

The grass tree (*Xanthorrhoea australis)*
Photograph by Trisha Dixon

The first garden created in Australia by white settlers was at Sydney Cove in New South Wales. It was, of necessity, a vegetable garden. Convicts began digging it three days after the First Fleet arrived on 26 January 1788. Eleven ships of the First Fleet brought naval officers, marines and

The first garden established by the new settlers at Sydney Cove in 1788
John Carmichael, 1803–1857
Detail from *Sydney N.S. Wales,* 1788
etching; 7.7 x 16.6 cm
From the Pictorial Collection

convicts to establish a settlement in New South Wales for strategic reasons and to help relieve the prisons of England of their excess of convicts. The Fleet brought with it stores, plants and seeds from England, supplemented by more plants and seeds collected at Cape Town and Rio de Janeiro on the

voyage out. The first need upon landing at Port Jackson was shelter and the second was food. Gardens and farms were quickly established to provide food for when the stores brought on the First Fleet ships were exhausted.

The second map of the settlement shows that within three months of their arrival, the settlers had established three gardens beside Sydney Cove and a farm over the ridge on Farm Cove. The map was drawn by Francis Fowkes, a convict from the First Fleet.

The beginnings of the colony of New South Wales were synonymous with botany. Explorers, many accompanied by professional or amateur botanists and artists, had collected and drawn the unique flora of the new lands in the Indian and Pacific Oceans and made them known to European and English scientists and amateur botanists.

Sir Joseph Banks and his botanical artists accompanied Captain Cook on his first voyage of exploration. Banks was a wealthy young man, a Fellow of the Royal Society, with connections to the politicians of Britain, who had a deep interest in botany and had already undertaken a voyage to

CHAPTER I

The First Garden

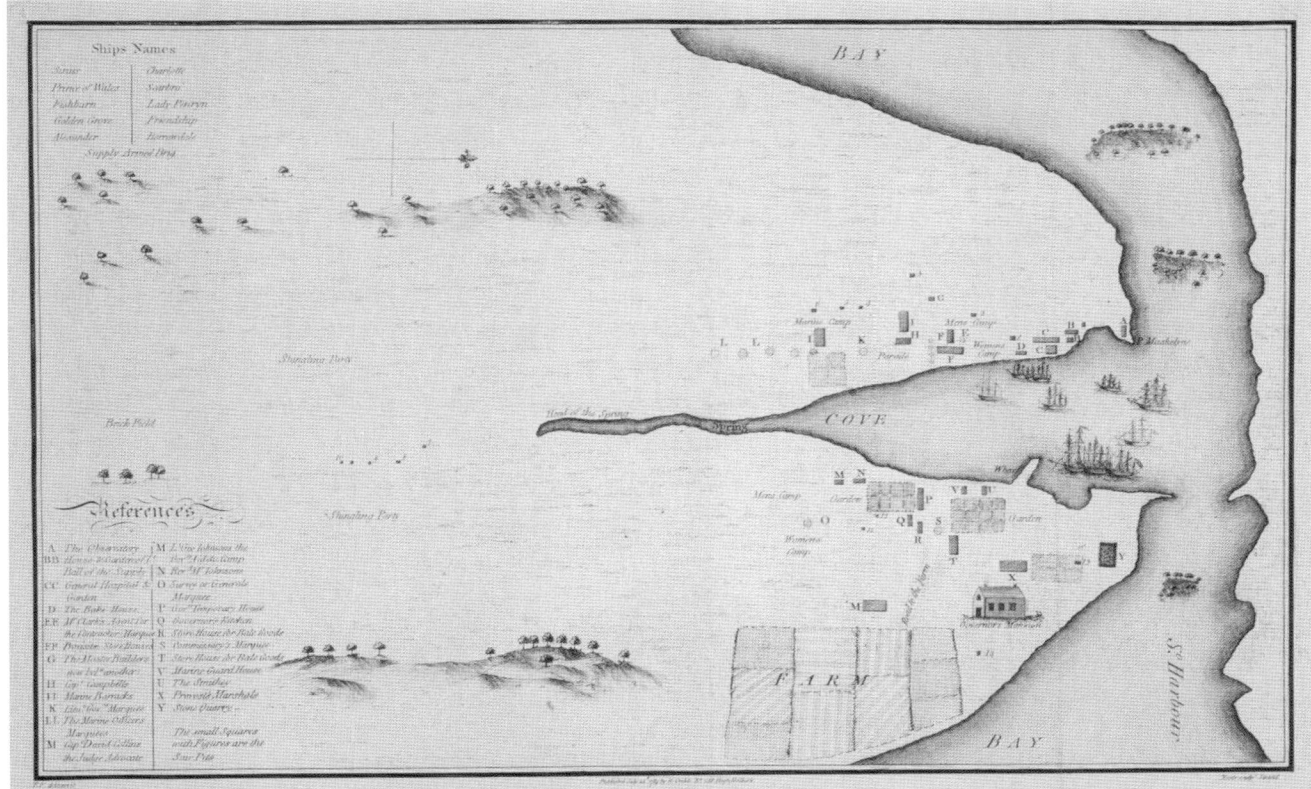

3

A map of the new settlement
at Sydney Cove

Francis Fowkes
*Sketch and Description of the Settlement
at Sydney Cove, Port Jackson in
the County of Cumberland Taken by a
Transported Convict*, 1789
hand coloured engraving; 19.5 x 31.6 cm
Rex Nan Kivell Collection;
from the Pictorial Collection

The First Garden

[to keep even a garden]
[...of the deepest concern.
...ctober our weekly allowance of provisions,
...been eight pounds of flour, five pounds of salt [...]
...of pease, six ounces of butter, was reduced to five po...
...ounces of flour, three pounds five ounces of pork, and [...]
...ts of pease.
In order to lessen the consumption from the public stores, [...]
...pply was ordered to touch at Lord Howe Island, in her way
...om Norfolk Island, to try if turtle could be procured, for th[...]
purpose of being publicly served in lieu of salt provisions. Bu[...]
...he brought back only three turtles, which were distributed in th...
...arrison.
December, 1789. At the request of his excellency, lieutenan[...]
...ces of the marines, accompanied by lieutenant Johnston a...
...Lowes, about this time undertook the attempt to cros[...]
...river, and to penetrate to Carmarthen mountains, [...]
...ed a ford in the river, they passed it, and pro[...]
...rection. But they found the country [...]
...adding so excessive, that in thi[...]
...e fifteen miles, and a[...]

Watkin Tench,
an officer in the
marines, describes
the difficulties in
obtaining supplies

Lines reproduced
from
*A Complete Account of
the Settlement*
by Watkin Tench
(London: G. Nicol,
1793)

Newfoundland and South Labrador. His reports of the land Cook named New South Wales were influential in the decision to establish the colony. Also of interest to a sea-going nation whose naval supplies of mast timbers and materials for sails were threatened by international crises were the reports of the strategic value of New Zealand flax (*Phormium tenax*) and the Norfolk Island pine (*Araucaria heterophylla*).

On arrival at Botany Bay, so-named by Cook in recognition of the botanical richness he and Banks discovered in 1770, Commodore Arthur Phillip, the first Governor of New South Wales, found it unsuitable as a place to settle and chose instead the huge harbour, Port Jackson, immediately to the north.

In those first years supplies were limited; the colony almost starved. Supply ships were sent infrequently from Britain and some of them sank on the voyage out. It was the historian Geoffrey Blainey who noted that distance was as characteristic of Australia as mountains are of Switzerland and it was because of the great distances separating the settlement from even the nearest Dutch colonies in the East Indies that alternative sources of supplies were so difficult to get.

The settlers depended on the stores they brought with them, the food they could grow and, until their stock of cattle increased, on hunting and fishing. But it wasn't long before they had fished out the harbour waters near them and lost some of their cattle in the bush. They supplemented what food they had by gathering indigenous plants, such as the native currant and leaves of seashore plants such as sea celery and New Zealand spinach (despite its name, an Australian plant), which Captain Cook had used to help prevent scurvy among his crews. Although the diversity of Australia's flora had created enormous interest in Europe, its usefulness, outside these examples, was still largely unknown.

Because the Aboriginal Australians were seen only as hunter gatherers, their knowledge of plants was discounted. However evidence is mounting that they did manage plants. Fire was used for a variety of purposes. In Cape York, for example, one use of fire is thought to have been to clear competing vegetation away from the cycads whose seeds were a staple food (although poisonous until treated). Fire also stimulated seed production. The Aborigines of Cape York limited the exploitation of yams such as ka-aatha and thampu and replanted the productive top of the tuber. Aborigines were also thought to plant seeds of wattles and other plants used for food along the trails they followed. Despite all this, their knowledge of plants was not understood or put to general use by the new settlers.

Among the problems confronting the settlers were the relative poorness of the soil compared to that in their home countries and the confounding climate. Further, much of the seed deteriorated on

the long voyage out and unfortunately, no-one thought to provide Governor Phillip with gardeners. This seems almost inexplicable, particularly as Banks had employed a gardener and an assistant to sail in the HMS *Bounty* to collect bread fruit from Tahiti at about the time the First Fleet was being assembled.

In May 1788, HMS *Supply* was despatched to get turtles from Lord Howe Island for the colony which was already running out of supplies. And in 1790, HMS *Sirius,* together with HMS *Supply,* was sent to Norfolk Island with marines and more than 200 convicts to reduce the strain on the starving colony. According to Watkin Tench, an invitation from a 'lucky man who had knocked down a dinner with his gun, or caught a fish by angling from the rocks, [and] invited a neighbour to dine with him, always ran "Bring your own bread"'.

In a letter to Lord Sydney, Secretary of the Home Department, in November 1788, Governor Phillip writes that the oranges, figs, apples and vines he had brought from Brazil were thriving and in his garden, vegetables were plentiful including cauliflowers and French beans, and strawberries from the Cape of Good Hope. But the fruit trees were some years off

Extensive vegetable gardens of the first Government House

William Bradley, c.1757–1833
View of the Governor's House at Sydney in Port Jackson, New South Wales, 1791
watercolour; 21.6 x 36 cm
From the Pictorial Collection

5

Productive gardens
surround the
houses on
Sydney Cove

Edward Dayes,
1763–1804
*South View of the
Town of Sydney,*
1797
watercolour;
17.5 x 24.2 cm
From the Pictorial
Collection

bearing and there were not enough vegetables to feed the colony.

Robert Bruce,
c.1835–1908
Detail from
*The Norfolk Pines
in the Botanical
Gardens, Sydney*
in *Illustrated Sydney
News,* 1872
wood engraving;
19 x 11.2 cm
From the Pictorial
Collection

William Bradley, first officer of the *Sirius,* produced one of the first watercolour paintings of the settlement. His *View of the Governor's House,* painted in 1791, shows the rectangular and square beds of a utilitarian garden where vegetables are the prime produce. The symmetrical central path is edged with what might be shrubs or food plants. The terrace is also utilitarian, a place for the marine guards and for guns pointing at the Cove. By 1792 elements of decoration had crept in showing that

conditions were easing. There are two round planted beds on the terrace, and round beds interrupt the ordered vegetable garden. Young trees, possibly fruit trees, are growing in the centre of each bed. A Norfolk Island pine (*Araucaria heterophylla*), with its distinctive silhouette, is planted to one side of the garden. It had been brought back for the Governor by one of the ships visiting Norfolk Island.

While most of the plants and seeds brought to New South Wales in the First Fleet were for food production, some decorative plants were also brought out. For example, Surgeon Bowes Smyth brought the hardy geranium (*Pelargonium* spp.), together with grape vines. They prospered in the poor and arid soil.

The droughts of the 1790s and the long periods between supply ships from Britain and India meant that supplies were almost at zero on a number of occasions, but gradually matters improved. By the time the watercolour *South View of the Town of Sydney* was painted in 1797 the colony was no longer in desperate straits. The ordered garden beds in front of many of the houses are still mainly planted with

Lawns, shrubs and trees make a decorative
garden at Government House. This aquatint
has been engraved by John Heaviside Clark
from an original work by John Eyre

John Heaviside Clark, c.1770–1863
New South Wales, View of Sydney from the East
Side of the Cove, 1810
hand coloured aquatint; 41.2 x 55.2 cm
Rex Nan Kivell Collection;
from the Pictorial Collection

vegetables, but the garden of Government House was becoming more decorative than productive.

The first gardens of the settlers were very plain and laid out in geometric order. They were at one with the unadorned Georgian architecture of the first houses. Vines, though grown for the grapes, introduced a decorative element as they clothed the walls of the houses.

By early in the new century, the garden of Government House showed that subsistence was no longer the sole preoccupation of the people living in the colony. In *New South Wales, View of Sydney from*

A Norfolk Island pine marks the site of Government House

J.W. Lewin, 1770–1819
View of Sydney Looking South, c.1811
watercolour;
32.4 x 58.5 cm
Rex Nan Kivell Collection;
from the Pictorial Collection

the East Side of the Cove, the artist shows how the grounds of Government House have developed. The vegetable gardens have given way to shrubs and grass. A garden bed is surrounded by a path. The Norfolk Island pine is already a stately height. In the background houses can be seen still surrounded by geometric beds of vegetables.

Governor Bligh, in his brief and troubled term of office, contributed to a transition in style that became evident elsewhere in the colony. He redesigned the ordered garden of Government House to one in the picturesque style. John Lewin's watercolour shows lawns sweeping down to the water, native trees on the left of the house providing a park-like setting, and a decorative stand of trees in the middle of the lawn. The distinctive outline of the Norfolk Island pine marks the site. The picket fence is no longer visible and a stone or cement wall runs along the Cove's edge.

Less than twenty years after the settlement was established in Sydney there was leisure time and more freedom from the demands of food production to think about the decorative design of gardens. Admittedly, the Governor's residence would have the trappings of a decorative garden before other houses, but as one of the most painted and drawn sites it gives us an indication of the progress of the new colony.

In England, the picturesque style which Governor Bligh adopted succeeded the landscape style. Though both styles appear somewhat similar to us, they differed from each other in detail. Indeed, the picturesque is regarded by some as more an intellectual concept than a style. However, both styles were in opposition to the formal garden—the artificial, the straight line, the parterre and topiary—and both styles imitated nature. They were informal, 'natural' and curvilinear, though classical 'incidents' such as temples were allowed. They were more suited to large and medium-sized gardens rather than small gardens, though a clever designer could adapt them to a smaller space.

The picturesque differed from the landscape style in that more formality was allowed close to the house and in wilder elements such as grottoes, waterfalls and chasms. Both styles were, of course, contrived. In England, whole villages were moved by some designers to create the effect they wanted; the art was in making them seem natural. Both styles were described by Nan Fairbrother as 'the simple life in satin slippers'. Possibly

Major James Taylor drew the productive cottage garden beside the Military Hospital, Sydney. Later in London the engraver, Robert Havell, added the foreground flowers

Robert Havell, 1769–1832
Detail from
The Entrance of Port Jackson and Part of the Town of Sydney, 1823
hand coloured aquatint; 47.8 x 65 cm
Rex Nan Kivell Collection; from the Pictorial Collection

One of the larger houses built in the new colony with a garden in the picturesque style. This engraving is based on an original work by John Eyre

W. Preston
View of the Seat of Woolloomoola [sic], *near Sydney in New South Wales*, 1813
engraving; 29.1 x 42 cm
Rex Nan Kivell Collection; from the Pictorial Collection

Robert Campbell's garden on the west side of Sydney Cove

Reproduced from
An Historical Account of the Colony of New South Wales and its Dependent Settlements
by James Wallis (London: R. Ackermann, 1821)
Plate II

work by John Eyre. It shows a developed garden with a carriage drive. Nature is tamed in that many trees have been cut and the bush has retreated behind the house. Some trees are left standing decoratively in the grass. A substantial fence and gates enclose the sides and back of the house. Lewin's engraving of 'the seat of Ultimo' also shows a garden in the picturesque style.

James Wallis's aquatint of the Cove from Dawes' Point shows the garden of Robert Campbell next to his house and behind his wharfage on the west side of Sydney Cove. The garden is shielded from the wharf buildings by a row of what appear to be stables. Earlier this garden was, like others, laid down to vegetables. But by this time the geometric beds, surrounded by paths, contain grass, shrubs and trees. It has become a 'gentleman's' garden.

the artists' impressions of Australia's natural landscape contributed more to the picturesque style in the early paintings than did the actual design.

About the same time as Lewin painted his watercolour of Government House, the *View of the Seat of Woolloomoola* [sic], *near Sydney in New South Wales* was engraved from an original

11

The picturesque-style garden of
Woolloomooloo House with the
borrowed landscape of the harbour

Sigismond Himely, 1801–1872
Vooloo-Moloo au Port Jackson,
c.1835
aquatint; 28.8 x 38.2 cm
Rex Nan Kivell Collection;
from the Pictorial Collection

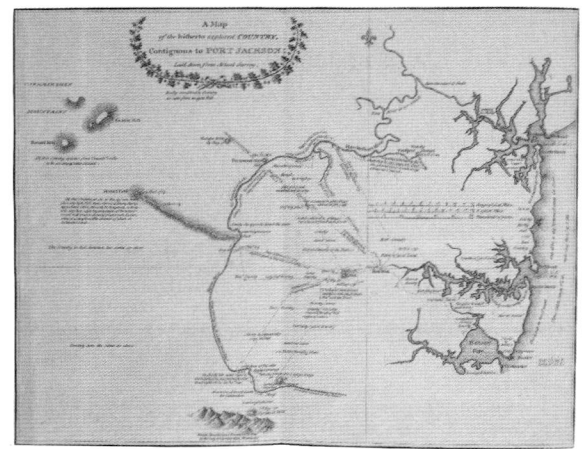

A further record of the very early gardens of Sydney comes from Major James Taylor who was posted to Sydney, arriving in 1817. His panorama of Sydney and Port Jackson appears in three published aquatints. In the grounds of the Military Hospital there is a cottage and outhouses. Vines grow on the wall of the cottage and stately flowers line the fence. A convict labours in the vegetable garden, officers chat between the cottage, kitchen and wash house, a lady, child and servant walk along the path, a kangaroo and fowls graze, and a dog supervises convicts moving wood. Labour and leisure mix. To the right are the formal grounds of the hospital with picket fences, sentry boxes and regular plantings of trees along the fence and formal paths. In the background are the picturesque grounds of Government House. The houses on the slopes to the south of Government House show four geometric layouts.

Just how close the artists' images are to the early gardens is impossible to say. Clearly, some of the features described above have been imposed by the engraver in England, for after comparing Major Taylor's original watercolours and the engravings made from them, it is apparent that the flowers in the foreground and the layout of some of the distant gardens were added in London, perhaps to make the scene more attractive. Another indication that we should not rely on all the observations of the early artists is in the drawings of eucalypts with their leaves standing up instead of hanging down. It is possible that the picturesque aspect of paintings and engravings such as the one of Woolloomooloo may have been imposed by the painter rather than the gardener. However, the French artist Sigismond Himely's view of Woolloomooloo shows a picturesque garden too.

Joseph Lycett's views may be somewhat more reliable as he added text to support his paintings which record the colony at the end of its third decade. Lycett was a portrait and miniature painter transported for forgery. But we cannot be entirely sure that he too did not impose the English view of the landscape on the Australian setting.

By the end of the third decade the range of buildings and gardens had increased. There were stately colonial Georgian and Regency villas scattered around the harbour, and the Governor's house at Rose Hill and the Parramatta settlement showed some signs of maturity.

Lycett's *View of Captain Piper's Naval Villa at Eliza Point near Sidney* [sic] shows a picturesque garden around a Colonial Regency house. Other views of this garden show that behind the house was a vegetable garden surrounded by a picket fence in a cruciform

Captain Piper's garden on the shores of Port Jackson is picturesque in style with a mixture of indigenous and exotic plants

Joseph Lycett, c.1775–1828 Detail from *View of Captain Piper's Naval Villa at Eliza Point near Sidney* [sic], *New South Wales*, 1825 hand coloured aquatint; 23 x 33 cm Rex Nan Kivell Collection; from the Pictorial Collection

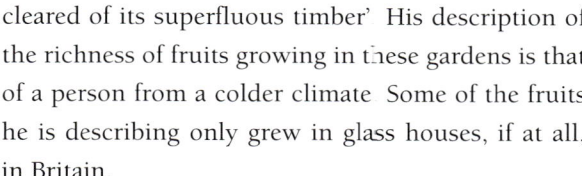

The wilderness made picturesque. Bushland has been cleared to make a garden around Burwood Villa, which lay between Sydney Cove and Rose Hill

Joseph Lycett, c.1775–1828 *Burwood Villa, New South Wales, the Property of Alexander Riley Esqr.,* 1825 hand coloured aquatint; 25.2 x 33 cm From the Pictorial Collection

shape. The house was shaded by eucalypts and casuarinas, and oranges, peaches, apricots and nectarines grew behind it. The garden of Burwood Villa is in the picturesque style. But the wildness of the surrounding country, some distance from the main settlement, necessitates an inner fence around the house. The style was achieved at a price, for as Lycett notes, 'it is a remarkable instance how speedily the forest in New South Wales can be

cleared of its superfluous timber' His description of the richness of fruits growing in these gardens is that of a person from a colder climate Some of the fruits he is describing only grew in glass houses, if at all, in Britain.

So from a starving colony in 1788, by its third decade the colony's gardens were exciting interest because of the diversity of their plants. The first botanical garden had been established at Rose Hill, followed by the gardens which became the Royal Botanic Gardens, Sydney. The first nursery had been established by Thomas Shepherd near the site of the future University of Sydney and its first stocks had been obtained from the gardens already established in the colony.

Though the gardens in the towns of Sydney and Parramatta were still largely geometric in layout, the English picturesque style is represented in the paintings and engravings of the larger gardens. At Government House, the vegetable garden started three days after the First Fleet arrived had become an elegant garden.

The Garden Grows

Nineteenth-century garden
created by Australian author and botanical illustrator
Louisa Meredith (1812–1895)

Spring Vale, Swansea, Tasmania
Photograph by Trisha Dixon

It was on the coast of this timeless and inhospitable land with its arid soil, hostile climate and variation in conditions that the new settlers and convicts began to spread and to garden. Most came from the cities and towns of England and Ireland where many people had no garden to speak of, living in terrace houses that opened straight onto the street. If there was a backyard, it was often a tiny, dank, shaded place for the privy and the coal. Only in the country were gardens common, and even then many cottagers lacked the land or the resources to invest in them.

In the colonies, of course, there was no such shortage of land, and it was Governor Phillip who was responsible for a tradition that endured till recently—that of the quarter acre block. Just what influenced him to nominate this size is not completely clear, though, at the time, planners developing model villages in England were recommending this as a good size for a cottage garden: a block with enough space around the cottage for the household to grow their own vegetables and later some decorative plants.

New gardens in the settlement of Newcastle

Sophia Campbell, 1777–1833
Newcastle with Christ Church in the Distance, c.1820
watercolour;
22.8 x 57.8 cm
From the Pictorial Collection

Victor Crittenden in his book, *The Front Garden*, has observed that the front garden was seen as a right for the early settlers, and that 'the first garden cities were actually Australian cities in practice if not in idea'.

The separated garden spaces shown in the previous chapter 'The First Garden' are also reflected in Sophia Campbell's drawings around Sydney and Newcastle, the new colony founded in 1801 at the mouth of the Hunter River. Sophia Campbell, the first woman artist in Australia and wife of the merchant Robert Campbell, painted Newcastle between 1818 and 1820. Picket fences march over the landscape demarcating each plot. Newcastle looks rather like a new suburban tract on the edge of a modern city. This is because of the size of each block.

Though the settlement of Hobart was not established until 1803, the first planting of exotic species on the island occurred in 1773 when Furneaux, one of Cook's companions, planted two seedling apples and some fruit kernels. On his last voyage of exploration Cook visited the site, Adventure Bay, to ascertain their fate. It was no

surprise then that apples were among the first trees planted by the settlers who found a climate far more like Britain than any part of the continent of Australia. As was the case in Sydney, the early years were times of difficulty and the emphasis was on subsistence. The journal of the Reverend Robert Knopwood, the first chaplain of Hobart, describes his very successful garden through the difficult times from 1804 to prosperity for the settlement in 1838. By 1807, in fact, there was a glut of potatoes. He was generous with the produce, giving it to the Governor, to friends, to people in need and to visiting ships. From the ships he received in return seeds, fruit stones and trees from the ships' landfalls elsewhere, including New Zealand. By 1814 he describes in his

Picket fences delineate boundaries of gardens yet to be established

Sophia Campbell, 1777–1853
Newcastle, c.1820
watercolour;
22.8 x 57.8 cm
From the Pictorial Collection

journal growing grass and shrubs and thenceforward his garden became a decorative as well as a productive one.

By the time Joseph Lycett visited Tasmania to paint the new settlement, there were many established gardens. Unhappily, his paintings do not show them in detail. One of his prints of the Roseneath Ferry shows a fenced garden on the banks of the Tamar River and areas of thick growth. possibly orchards, to one side.

One of the early large gardens in Tasmania, which in 1996 is being restored by the National Trust and Richard Ratcliffe, a Canberra landscape architect, is Highfield, the home of the first manager of the Van Diemen's Land Company. The garden, first painted in about 1835, is shown as a picturesque landscape. Cows are grazing in the foreground, as in so many paintings of European landscapes, but in the middle distance are a pair of kangaroos and two emus (the latter now extinct in Tasmania).

Another painting (not shown) of Highfield in the Allport Library in Hobart, dated 1840, presents a different aspect of the garden. It shows the garden in the gardenesque style—a style which had recently become fashionable in England. Paths outline the stiff garden beds newly planted with young conifers, and a deciduous tree, possibly a birch, is shown in one corner. There is a grape and a rose on the wall near the house and flowers and young shrubs. A drive and lookout is to the front of the house.

Cleared landscape and fenced garden of an early settlement near Hobart

Joseph Lycett, c.1775–1828
Detail from *Roseneath Ferry, near Hobart Town, Van Diemens Land,* 1824
hand coloured aquatint;
23.5 x 33 cm
Rex Nan Kivell Collection; from the Pictorial Collection

A picturesque landscape garden in Tasmania. By 1840 this garden was being redesigned in the new gardenesque style

Artist unknown *Highfield, Circular Head, Stanley, Tasmania, Residence for Edward Curr First Manager of the Van Diemen's Land Company,* c.1835
oil on canvas;
25.3 x 30.5 cm
Rex Nan Kivell Collection; from the Pictorial Collection

The two paintings of Highfield mark the transition point from the picturesque to the gardenesque style. This latter style is attributed to John Claudius Loudon, an English garden writer and publisher. Loudon popularised gardening as an art partly to help improve the human condition, founding *The Gardener's Magazine* in 1826 for this purpose. Through the magazine and his other writings, his designs and theories became known.

He considered that a garden should be recognised as a work of art, not an imitation of nature. He believed that the display of the characteristics of an individual plant was of more importance than the overall garden scheme. Flower gardens formerly banished to the extremities of a pleasure ground were installed around villa residences. The introduction of many 'new' plants and shrubs from overseas, including Australia, was another impetus towards the gardenesque style. Many of the tender plants from abroad could not withstand the British climate so were housed in glasshouses. Arboretums, herbariums and pinetums to display collections became fashionable. The gardenesque style could be adapted to any size garden from the smallest to the

largest and it quickly attracted the people of Victorian Britain. Australian gardens followed.

In Tasmania the botanical gardens were started in 1829, enclosed by two substantial walls which served

as protection from the Roaring Forties. And in 1836 the first-known Australian nursery catalogue was produced in Hobart. It was printed in the *Hobart Town Courier* and listed trees, shrubs, perennials, bulbs and vegetables. It listed some Australian plants starting with *Acacia* spp., *Eucalyptus* spp. ('all the varieties'—a large claim by the author), *Hakea*, three species of *Casuarina* and other common indigenous

Eucalypts provide the main canopy for this early Western Australian garden
H.W. Reveley, 1788–1875
My House and Garden in Western Australia, 1833
watercolour;
25.1 x 39.8 cm
Rex Nan Kivell Collection; from the Pictorial Collection

plants. Lists, such as this one, can be helpful when identifying plants used at a particular time.

One of the first gardens depicted in Western Australia is the garden of Henry Reveley, its first engineer and architect. In his own drawing, which was included in a letter to England in 1833, he shows a garden which was partly utilitarian, partly decorative. A drive leads from the road. Ducks are 'posting off to a duck pond behind those trees' and 'the tail water, where there is always a dribble of water' has a wash house placed over it. Some kind of a scoop hangs over the water below. The flower and vegetable gardens are enclosed by a brush fence. Reveley's vegetable garden is laid out in geometric order. It contains cabbages, cauliflowers and onions and a separate potato bed. Decorative plants are in flower beds inside the enclosure, and there are vines and a tree mallow at the corner of the house. This garden owes less to any particular garden style than to a response to practical need. Outside the enclosed space, the garden has a spacious relaxed air about it.

In Victoria in 1845, Duncan Cooper, the son of Major General George Cooper who had served in India, painted his house at Challicum. Two views show different aspects of the garden. One shows something between a moat and a ha-ha (with a bridge over it) to keep out stock. Possibly an eroded creek bed, the ha-ha served the purpose of an unobtrusive fence. The painting shows garden beds and a eucalypt in the foreground. The other view, from the window of the house, shows the geometric layout of the garden beds more clearly and the way the ha-ha divides the garden

An eroded creek bed creates a natural ha-ha in this garden

Duncan Cooper, c.1813–1904
Third Hut, Challicum, 1845
watercolour;
14.8 x 21.7 cm
From the Pictorial Collection

No visual barrier separates this
charming cottage garden from the
surrounding landscape

Duncan Cooper, c.1813–1904
*View from Window of Hut,
Challicum*, 1850
watercolour;
15.4 x 25 cm
From the Pictorial Collection

and house from the panorama. No effort has been made to block out the view or to isolate the viewer from it, in contrast to many gardens where the fence protected the house and shielded the occupants from the wide open spaces.

An exquisite album of watercolours by an artist known only by the initials E.T. shows several properties in the New England district of New South Wales in the 1840s. Moredun near the Macintyre River has a well-established garden. The drive is of dirt or gravel. There are a number of garden beds filled with shrubs and bamboos. Climbers on the verandah provide shade and the whole image gives an appearance of lushness even though there are no lawns.

In about 1853 Jane Dorothea Cannan drew an established cottage and garden such as one might see on the edge of country towns today. It stands on a slight rise with a comfortable verandah shielded by a trellis that does not obscure the view. A eucalypt guards the cottage to the front and eucalypts surround it at the back. Climbers give added shade on the verandah and shrubs edge the wire and timber fence which cuts the garden off from the track to the outhouses behind the cottage. This is a timeless image.

A lush garden at Moredun in the New England district of New South Wales

E.T.
Moredun from the Garden, c.1848
watercolour;
18.4 x 24.5 cm
Rex Nan Kivell Collection;
from the Pictorial Collection

Although drawn in the 1850s, this cottage and garden could be seen in a country town today

Jane Dorothea Cannan, 1823–1861
Country Cottage, c.1853
pencil; 17 x 26.1 cm
From the Pictorial Collection

Clearly, gardens had become havens in this wide brown land. Major Mitchell, returning in 1836 from one of his long journeys and surveys of the south-east of Australia reached the district of the new town of Goulburn, 193 kilometres from Sydney, after seven months of exploration in previously unknown lands and he gratefully records:

> I had arrived in a country which I myself had surveyed, and where the roads and towns in progress were the first fruits of these labours ... I reached at twilight the house of a worthy friend, Captain Rossi, who received me with great kindness and hospitality ... A walk in the garden; a visit to the shearing shed; the news of colonial affairs in general; fat pullets cooked à la gastronome, and some good wine; had each in their turn rare charms for me.

CHAPTER 3
Through the Artist's Eye

One of the most ancient of plants,
the King protea *(Protea cynaroides)* dates back 300 million years
to the super continent of Gondwana before it broke up to form
Australia, Africa, South America, New Zealand and New Guinea

Photograph by Trisha Dixon

The discovery of gold in New South Wales and Victoria in 1851 signalled the beginning of a period of profound change in the social, economic and political structure of the colonies, and the rising affluence of the free settlers was reflected in their gardens in the rapidly expanding towns and on the established properties. Free migration had been strongly promoted in the 1830s and 1840s and the

A gardener with his scythe, the tool used to cut grass prior to the invention of the lawn-mower

G.E. Peacock, 1806–?
Craig End, Sydney, NSW, c.1850
oil on academy board;
25.2 x 34.8 cm
Rex Nan Kivell Collection;
from the Pictorial Collection

discovery of gold provided a powerful incentive for many thousands more to follow. Among them were gardeners, nurserymen, botanists and trained garden designers; professionals who were able to benefit from the lessons of climate, soil and season that had been learnt the hard way by the early settlers.

The new gardenesque style was popular, but the influx of migrants from diverse backgrounds brought with it an infusion of influences which produced an eclecticism that can be seen in many Australian gardens today. While the English garden tradition continued to be the dominant influence, there were a number of other influences, including that brought to Australia by army officers who had served in India, and who were more familiar with harsh climates and wide landscapes than those who came directly from Europe—and less inclined to screen off the house and garden from the great spaces outside.

Not surprisingly, plants and trees introduced from Europe did better in colonies that had common climatic features. In the warmer parts of the continent, it was the hardy plants acquired from South America and Africa on the long journey from Britain that did particularly well, perhaps reflecting the shared geological past of the three continents. Along with India, New Guinea and New Zealand, they once made up the super continent of Gondwana, probably explaining the striking

Hardy plants withstand the salt-laden winds in this Western Australian garden

Henry James Warre, 1819–1898
School House at King George Sound, W. Australia, 1860
watercolour;
14 x 20 cm
Rex Nan Kivell Collection; from the Pictorial Collection

similarities between plants, like the African proteas and the Australian waratah, and their ability to thrive, making possible the rich mix of indigenous and exotic plants in so many early gardens.

Henry Warre's watercolour of the School House at King George Sound in Western Australia shows a garden full of hardy succulents and cacti, *Strelitzia* spp., *Agave stricta*, eucalypts and native shrubs

which stand up to the harsh salt-laden winds from the Antarctic. The house is reminiscent of India and of Cheltenham in England, home of many retired Indian officers.

In this period before photography, many artists roamed the country painting houses and gardens for the proud owners. George French Angas was an artist who enjoyed recording the gardens as well as the houses of the rich and the new middle class. One

of his drawings shows a rampant prickly pear (*Opuntia* spp.) which became a scourge to grazing lands in tropical areas of Australia. Brought here by the First Fleet, it was just one of the introduced species which slowly naturalised and became a major problem. Others are the briar (*Rosa canina*), the olive in South Australia and the bitou bush along the New South Wales coastline. (Ironically, the attractive bitou bush, possibly introduced to Melbourne as a garden plant, is displacing the indigenous *Acacia longifolia* and in South Africa, the home of the bitou bush, it is being threatened by the introduced *Acacia longifolia*.)

The German painter Eugene von Guerard came to the Victorian goldfields in search of gold in the 1850s but he soon resumed painting which he had studied with his father, also a painter. He had many commissions to paint settlers' homes. His houses and gardens are on a grand scale and set in sweeping landscapes.

One of the best-known colonial painters, S.T. Gill, was also working during this period. In his paintings he depicted almost every aspect of life from gold mining to exploration, from sport to Aborigines. He also painted

houses and gardens. In many of these he captures the gardener at work with his equipment and records the garden seasons of the year.

As these images show, many gardeners mixed styles and, of course, many developed their gardens with no thought of a unified design. Fashionable gardenesque-style gardens, large formal gardens, cottage gardens and gardens of no particular style existed side by side. In many cases, they were influenced by writings and illustrations from overseas or by the horticultural journals and newspaper gardening columns that were published locally. Sometimes those fortunate to travel abroad brought back ideas with them. By late in the nineteenth century gardening was a popular subject and horticultural societies were being established.

In the interests of garden history, some of the surviving gardens of the nineteenth

Tropical plants enclosed by immaculately clipped edging

Yandilla Station, Queensland
From the Pictorial Collection

far left
Establishing a garden in the virgin soil
S.T. Gill, 1818–1880
Spring, c.1847
watercolour;
29.3 x 21.8 cm
From the Pictorial Collection

left
A rose flourishes in this settler's garden
S.T. Gill, 1818–1880
March, c.1847
watercolour;
21.8 x 18.2 cm
From the Pictorial Collection

Box hedge along the
carriageway in 1859
Durham Hall, Braidwood,
New South Wales
From the Pictorial
Collection

The same carriageway
more than a
century later
Durham Hall, Braidwood,
New South Wales
Photograph by
Trisha Dixon

century have been studied. Olive and Dick Royd's Durham Hall on the harsh plains of the Braidwood area of New South Wales is one of these. Their garden is basically a Victorian garden which has only been modified over the years to accommodate extensions to the house and the death of major trees. It is thought that the first part of the garden was planted in the early 1840s. It was set out in a typical early Victorian style with symmetrically patterned box hedging detailing the carriage loop and nearby flower beds. Now the hedges have matured and

grown over much of the old drive which is no longer used. The present drive goes to the back of the house in typical country fashion. The front door is rarely opened. A huge Atlas cedar (*Cedrus atlantica* or possibly *Cedrus libani*) dominates the garden, the last of four planted symmetrically on the northern side of the carriage loop. A weeping funeral cypress (*Cupressus funebris*) had to be cut down after it developed a dangerous lean only a few years ago. Windbreaks of elms and hawthorns were planted to the west for protection against the searing westerlies and north-westerlies of spring, summer and winter. There once was a vista from the front door through the concentric circles of the drive hedges past the cedars to a distant hill on which Lombardy poplars were planted as a terminus to the view but the mature garden now obscures much of this. There is a billowing hedge of roses and an enormous wisteria spreads across garages and sheds and climbs into the upper branches of a pine.

This garden shows the result of plants achieving their ultimate size, a problem few of us have to face in our lifetime. It also presents a conservation problem: should the box hedges, for example, be replaced by cuttings struck from the original plantings to make it once again the size the first gardener imagined or should the plants be allowed to live their normal life cycle?

The garden is full of unusual plants which, with changing fashions are no longer available from nurseries, such as an Osage orange

left
Inedible fruit from a favourite colonial hedging plant, Osage orange (*Maclura pomifera*)
Photograph by Trisha Dixon

below
Newly established gardens in the cleared landscape
François Cogné, 1829–1883
Buninyong, Victoria, c.1859
lithograph;
27.7 x 44 cm
From the Pictorial Collection

31

(*Maclura pomifera*) and *Desmodium amethystinum* from Chile. There are a number of unidentified roses, including a yellow one planted around 1880.

The artists and amateur painters captured many historic scenes. Binnum Binnum painted by Stanley Leighton is a wonderful record from settlement to

Evolution of the Australian homestead and garden from slab hut to Victoriana and from dirt track to gravel paths

Stanley Leighton, 1837–1901
Binnum Binnum, Mr H. Jones's, Tattiara Country, South Australia, 1868
watercolour; 8.7 x 33.5 cm
From the Pictorial Collection

prosperity in 1868. In the painting, the original slab hut is on the left and next to it is a pisé house which has been connected by a walkway to a new substantial Victorian house. The garden, too, reflects the stages of development: from the rough grass and dirt track on the left to a formal drive and garden

beds around the latest house. Stanley included this watercolour in his sketchbook and diary of a tour around South Australia in 1868. He records several services including communion for twenty at the homestead, a ball for seventy people and a kangaroo hunt in the weekend he was there.

In the boom period following the gold rushes, large and ornate houses in the Victorian Gothic style were built. Rupertswood, in Victoria, is a fine example. In 1874 there was a formal series of terraces and flights of steps descending the rise on which the house stood, but at the bottom there was a change of mood with a romantic pool overhung by willows.

Splendid photograph albums in the National Library of Australia's collection record many gardens. Photographs were taken by the owners of the garden, by visitors and by itinerant photographers—all of whom began to replace the artist as the recorder of Australian life. The Library has a photograph of 'A Station in the North West' taken by Charles Kerry. The eucalypts have been kept as a frame for this garden. There seems to be a mix of Australian and exotic plants, the white cedar (*Melia azedarach*), oleanders and something not unlike saltbush. The climbers on the

verandah are carefully shaped giving deep shade in the heat of the summer. While identifying plants from photographs or paintings is an uncertain business, if these plants are what we think they are, then this garden is particularly interesting because of the acceptance of the local flora.

Little is known about Australian garden designers of the nineteenth century except for William Guilfoyle. He was the son of an English landscape gardener who trained under the great Sir Joseph Paxton in Britain, gardener to the Duke of

Town house surrounded by cottage garden

Hardy Wilson, 1881–1955
Detail from *Davey Street, Hobart*, c.1918
pencil; 35.5 x 45.5 cm
From the Pictorial Collection

left
A Guilfoyle-designed landscape in the Western District of Victoria

Mawallok, Beaufort, Victoria
Photograph by Trisha Dixon

Architectural planting
typified by William
Guilfoyle
Mooleric, Birregurra,
Victoria
Photograph by
Trisha Dixon

Count Louis Delafosse, an adviser to Louis XIV on his gardens. In the late 1840s William Guilfoyle migrated to Australia with his father. At first he worked in the nursery his father established at Double Bay. In 1863 he undertook a voyage to the South Seas collecting plants and six years later he settled on the Tweed River in northern New South Wales, growing sugar cane, collecting local plants and establishing a tropical garden. Many of the plants he collected were sent to the Royal Botanic Gardens in Melbourne. In 1873 he succeeded Baron Ferdinand von Mueller as director of the gardens and set about transforming them.

In philosophy he followed the English school of landscaping: design should follow nature, not the formal lines of European gardens. He considered that landscape beauty had been sacrificed to correct geographical classification of plants and he changed the gardens considerably. The absence of lawns and the presence of 'unnatural' avenues of trees which resulted from von Mueller's work did not agree with his design philosophy. Like his father's mentor, Paxton, he moved many trees to achieve the effects he wanted; in the summer of 1874–75 he successfully moved 832 trees,

Devonshire. His grandfather was steward of the Tichborne estates and responsible for the splendid landscape gardens there. His mother's forebear was

Notable homestead garden in the gardenesque style

Rossiville, Goulburn, New South Wales
From the Pictorial Collection

The vibrant garden of the great
artist and intrepid traveller
Ellis Rowan

Ellis Rowan, 1848–1922
Ellis Rowan's Garden at Derriweit,
Mount Macedon, c.1885
watercolour; 28.6 x 18.4 cm
From the Pictorial Collection

losing only six. He deepened the lagoon to make it an ornament rather than the swampy marsh it formerly was. He used *Eucalyptus ficifolia* the Western Australian flowering gum, *Magnolia grandiflora*, rhododendrons and jacarandas (*Jacaranda mimosifolia*) to clothe the islands in the lagoon. He planted masses of annuals to provide much-needed colour. All this was done at first with shortages of staff and skilled supervisors.

He followed the same landscape style in his private garden designs. Sweeping wide lawns offset grand stands of trees and architectural plants, such as agaves, cordylines, yuccas and the Canary Islands palm, gave textural contrast.

Guilfoyle received both praise and blame for his work. Some considered he had failed, some that he had triumphed. He ignored both schools of thought. Finally, his designs using plants suited to Australian conditions were considered to be in the best traditions of the English landscape school. The ideas he put to work at the Royal Botanic Gardens in Melbourne and in his private garden designs influenced many people. It was his strong approach to design which has allowed much of his work to survive.

C H A P T E R   4
Back to Basics

The productive garden

Birchfield, Bungendore, New South Wales
Photograph by Trisha Dixon

Isolated bush cottage
from an album of
photographs *Victoria
through the Camera*,
taken about 1898

From the Pictorial
Collection

The cottage garden concept came to Australia with the first settlers but it evolved through a series of overlaid styles. Just as in Britain where among the flowers grew the vegetables for the family, including nettles (*Urtica dioica*) and dandelions (*Taraxacum* spp.), and where the fowls

40

scratched, the aim was to be productive as well as pretty. Although having some lawn was not unknown in English cottage gardens of the nineteenth century, it became far more dominant in Australia because of the space available. Later, the emphasis on outdoor living that began with the introduction of the private tennis court was accentuated with outdoor eating and the arrival of the swimming pool and barbeque.

Whether the land owner was affluent or poor, the theme of productivity was a common feature of early Australian gardens. Fresh vegetables were important and difficult to obtain and their presence is evident in the illustrations of gardens of large town houses and prosperous properties of the later nineteenth century, as well as those belonging to settlers who struggled through the depression of the 1890s.

Another gardening tradition that began in the nineteenth century is the Chinese market garden. Indeed, one which has been near the Cook's River, in Sydney, since last century is still worked by people who sell the produce locally.

Just as artists roamed the country mid-century, photographers began to travel through it later in the

Rudimentary productive garden Gippsland, Victoria

Photograph by Nicholas Caire From the Pictorial Collection

Formal kitchen garden Garangula, Harden, New South Wales Photograph by Trisha Dixon

century, recording not just the homes of the established and affluent but the houses of the new settlers as well. In the 1890s depression the gardens around new houses and humpies reverted to being subsistence or productive gardens. In one photograph from the period a woman with children sits in front of an L-shaped building, a house

right
Rural Solitude

Photograph by
Charles Kerry
Tyrrell Collection; from
the Pictorial Collection

below
Lilies, sunflowers,
daisies and pumpkin
flourish outside this
bush humpy

Photograph by
Charles Kerry
Tyrrell Collection; from
the Pictorial Collection

evidently built in stages. Parts of it are of undressed timber and parts are plastered over. The garden, laid out in neat beds, is well kept and vegetables grow in rows. Though modest it has an air of confidence.

Charles Kerry, who photographed many cottages and bushmen's huts, captured a bush humpy set against the cleared forest. Tall sunflowers, lilies and daisies

with a pumpkin ramping through them surround a slab hut with a bark roof. Another of his photographs, called Rural Solitude, shows a substantial, if crooked, fence surrounding the fertile garden of a hut. There are perennials in front of the house and roses climbing up the house and covering the hedge. A bush house—a stucture that protected delicate plants from the heat of the day and in cooler areas from frosts in winter—has a creeper over it. A gate made of thin straight branches closes the garden off but not, one thinks, for security rather to keep animals like the capering dog off the plants.

A homestead on the Cox River, which is much more prosperous, shows a substantial garden where eucalypts provide shelter, creepers cover the verandah and perennials surround it. Fruit trees are planted along the fences and vines are lined up on the

A productive
rural garden

Cox River,
New South Wales
Tyrrell Collection; from
the Pictorial Collection

Back to Basics

A substantial vegetable
garden on a pastoral station
in the 1890s

Coonong,
New South Wales
Photograph by
Sir Samuel McCaughey
S. McCaughey Collection;
from the Pictorial Collection

44

slope facing the sun. Grassy swathes and cattle plodding past complete a contented picture.

The large vegetable garden at Coonong, a McCaughey property in New South Wales, shows a garden that probably provided food for many of its workers. Grapes grow on the high and substantial fence, one which would keep out kangaroos. Fruit trees and vegetables, including globe artichokes, grow in well-ordered array. Gardeners would have been employed to tend this garden.

The head station of
Mr J. Balfe

*Buddabuddah, Bogan
River, New South Wales*
Reproduced from *Town
and Country Journal,*
1874
From the Pictorial
Collection

A neatly laid-out vegetable
garden in Hobart

H.J. Graham, 1858–1929
House and Garden, c.1884
watercolour; 10.2 x 20 cm
From the Pictorial Collection

46

Buddabuddah, on the Bogan River on the western plains of New South Wales, is shown in the *Town and Country Journal* for 1874. On a different scale to Coonong, it is nevertheless a neatly laid-out garden with vegetables towards the back and staked plants in the front. It is hard to tell whether they are vines or young fruit trees. A broad path crosses in front of the house. Picket fences and slightly more important gates secure the area from stock. The river flowing at the bottom of the garden would not have been as easily managed. Reduced to a trickle or less in dry seasons and to a flood in wet seasons, it would have been an uneasy companion. Because of the erratic nature of rivers, many settlers built their houses on higher land and grew their vegetables away from the house on the river flats. This was particularly the case with melons, which explains why wild melons can be found growing along many river courses today.

Harold Graham, who sketched many places in the eastern colonies in the 1880s, included a view of his own vegetable garden in Hobart. Of a different scale to those on the great properties, it is a carefully tended vegetable garden with cabbages and fruit trees in the foreground of the fine view.

left
The gardener's companion, Sir Nicholas Salix, handcrafted from willow by sculptor Pam Scott

The Old Bibbenluke Inn, Monaro, New South Wales
Photograph by Trisha Dixon

far left
Decorative kitchen garden

Valleyfield, Epping Forest, Tasmania
Photograph by Trisha Dixon

The growing number of productive, sustainable gardens today are not just a product of the back-to-the-earth movement, they are also descendants of these original cottage gardens. Indeed, just as was the case a century ago, many productive gardens with their herbs, vegetables and fruit trees are also gardens which are strikingly pretty

Expansive country vegetable garden with
antiquated wooden cottage once home to
a Chinese vegetable gardener

Woolongoon, Mortlake, Victoria
Photograph by Trisha Dixon

C H A P T E R   5
The Garden Designer

Edna Walling stonework

Bickleigh Vale, Mooroolbark, Victoria
Photograph by Trisha Dixon

far right
Landscaping advertisement featuring a drive in the garden of a Californian bungalow

Reproduced from *The Garden and Home Maker of Australia,* September 1927

THE RESIDENCE OF STANLEY E. PARRY, ESQ, OF BE-MORE

This is an actual Photograph of the grounds laid out by us which was taken three months after the time of laying the first Turf.
A photo of different Residences showing our work will appear in each issue of this journal.
Put the laying out of your grounds in capable hands.
Estimates for TURFING, PLANTING, ROCKWORK, TENNIS COURTS, TOP-DRESSING, in town or country (free).

BEAUMONT & CO.

The Leading Landscape Gardeners & Nurserymen   ·   ·   ·   BALTIMORE STREET, CAMPSIE

right and below
John D. Moore's design for a domestic garden in the mid-war period

Reproduced from *The Home,* June 1920

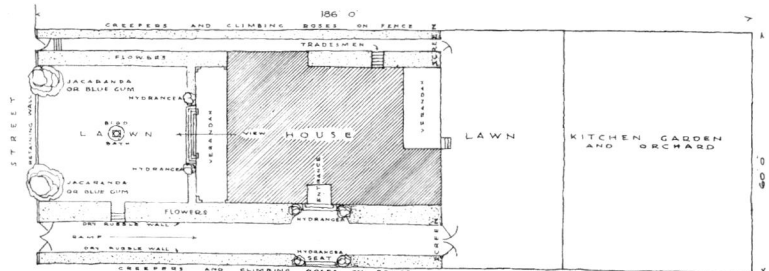

The beginning of the new century and the unification of the colonies into the federation of Australia was accompanied by an increase in the variety of house and garden styles. As cities extended and suburbs expanded, the quarter acre block remained the standard. Though the motor car was yet to exert its influence, the invention of the lawn-mower and the hose, toward the end of the nineteenth century, significantly affected gardens, making vast expanses of neatly trimmed grass possible for everyone.

While the gardenesque style continued into the new century, enhanced by the lawn which the lawn-mower had made possible, elements of it were adapted into a new style which became known as the Federation garden. In this garden the front path curved and the garden beds were plainer but not geometric—anything but straight. Garden ornaments, including fountains, birdbaths, cement statues and ornamental balustrades were featured and annuals with their bright colours came into prominence.

The geometric style also persisted. John D. Moore's design for a small garden reflected the preference of many households: the front garden is decorative although symmetrical and based on straight lines; the paths do not divide the lawn; one path runs down the side of the house to the tradesman's entrance, the back door; and the other path, wide enough for a car, leads to the main entrance on the other side of the house. Side entrances were in vogue for a while. On Moore's plan, the house was to be framed by jacarandas (*Jacaranda mimosifolia*) or blue gums (*Eucalyptus saligna*), both very large trees. Hydrangeas and flower beds lined both sides of the lawn and the paths. At the back, a lawn provided a recreation area and beyond it lay a kitchen garden and orchard.

Lloyd Rees drew an ideal house and garden of the 1920s in his engraving for the masthead of *The Home; an Australian Quarterly* which aimed to

Lloyd Rees's drawing of an ideal home

Reproduced from *The Home*, February 1920

introduce 'the best' in design. Again, trees frame the house. A curved path leads to the front door. Plants tumble over a low stone wall, separating the garden from the street, and climb up to the windows. The house is on show. There is no barrier such as a fence or hedge to obscure the view of passers-by. The front garden is not a useful garden like the cottage garden where the productive and the decorative mingle.

The bungalow garden of the 1920s was above all a garden featuring lawns. Couch or buffalo grass surrounded the house and typical plantings included wattle, cypress, jacaranda (*Jacaranda mimosifolia*) and citrus such as lemon, mandarin, orange and lime. Clipped privet hedges were also fashionable.

Roses became very popular about this time and their appeal has not waned since, though different types of roses come in and out of fashion. In many gardens, roses, particularly the bush tea roses, replaced the beds of annuals and other massed colourful plants. Rose-swathed pergolas and trellises and rose hedges became fashionable. The pink and red radiance roses, 'the best of the utility roses' were highly recommended, as were white Maman Cochet and yellow Safrano among others.

Another style which came back into fashion was the formal style. Coombe Cottage, Dame Nellie Melba's home in Melbourne, shows the formal, or classical influence, in her pool and terrace.

In 1920 William Hardy Wilson the architect and designer, drew a plan of a garden for the Ideal Australian Home Competition.

A swimming pool in the formal garden of Dame Nellie Melba's Coombe Cottage

Reproduced from *The Home*, February 1920

The Garden Designer

The front garden is classical Roman. The entrance is a straight path to a circular terrace which is built around an atrium, as in Roman houses. On either side of the path and terrace are stiff lines of cypress.

left
An ideal house and garden designed by Hardy Wilson. There is a mix of Roman and Australian elements in his design

Reproduced courtesy of Dr L. Hardy Wilson

far left
An idealised view of the front garden of a terrace house in Sydney

Hardy Wilson, 1881–1955
Richmond Terrace, Domain, Sydney, 1920
pencil; 45 x 35.1 cm
From the Pictorial Collection

AN IDEAL AUSTRALIAN HOME
PERSPECTIVE SKETCH.

Palms provide an architectural element in this garden on the Parramatta River

Hardy Wilson, 1881–1955
Newington, Parramatta River, NSW, 1916
pencil; 45.3 x 34.3 cm
From the Pictorial Collection

Straight trimmed hedges outline the path and the side tradesman's entrance. The circle of the terrace is repeated by a circular pool to one side. There is a terrace at the back of the house which overlooks a tennis court. Behind the tennis court is a wilderness area which might have been intended as an orchard and vegetable garden. This charming eclecticism is superimposed on a sketch of Sydney and its harbour.

Wilson's drawing of Newington, on the Parramatta River, shows foundation planting along the verandah rather in the American style. This is a lush planting in a formal style, slightly marred by one of a pair of palms having outgrown the other— a common problem for gardeners. The garden is rich in palms and bamboos set off by swathes of grass.

The American influence, which had been growing since the late 1800s, received an impetus from newspapers and magazines. But the dominant American influence came through films emanating from Hollywood. Harold Cazneaux's photograph of Shadowood, in Bowral, shows a south-west American influence in both the house and the courtyard. Crazy paving and a central pool make an open entrance courtyard. The cement-rendered walls

are offset by foundation plantings and fastigiate cypress, which make dramatic accents against the pale walls.

From the beginning, Australian gardens featured a mix of native and exotic, or introduced, plants but during the early years of the twentieth century the idea of creating gardens solely of native plants gained appeal. Amy Mack, who published several popular books on the bush and wrote in the *Sydney Morning*

The south-west American style is evident in both the house and courtyard of Shadowood, Bowral

Photograph by Harold Cazneaux
From the Pictorial Collection

Herald, was one of those who urged an appreciation of indigenous plants. In 1920 she published an account of one of the largest native and exotic gardens in Sydney, Tregoyd at Balmoral, which had been established in the 1890s.

Mack's account was published in the December edition of *The Home,* one of the journals encouraging the use of native plants. The same edition of the magazine featured Bilgoela, a seaside house with a large garden where the spectacular cabbage tree palms (*Livistona australis*) add drama to the scene.

right
Courtyard garden
Photograph by Harold Cazneaux
From the Pictorial Collection

below
Cabbage tree palms (*Livistona australis*) photographed by Harold Cazneaux
Bilgoela, New South Wales
Reproduced from *The Home,* December 1920

The HOME

THE AUSTRALIAN GARDEN AT "TREGOYD"

The quiet native lilies stand like sweet torches at the corner of this pathway which takes many pleasant glimpses of the Harbour.

The upper terrace, with pathway winding through local floras, shrubs, and trees, down to the extensive leisure garden.

A rustic seat beneath an overhanging rock, with native creepers and shrubs in their wild state.

A picturesque pathway through flowering bush shrubs and creepers

Page Thirty-two

Government House, Sydney. One wonders, perhaps, if the original source were Surgeon Bowes Smyth's geraniums which he brought with him on the First Fleet. Bilgoela is one garden where exotics and indigenous plants mixed to great effect.

Charles Weston, who planned the early plantings in Canberra, and Walter Burley Griffin, who designed the city, were also advocates of native plants and their concept of the city beautiful, the garden city, encompassed a desire to use native trees.

Another magazine, *The Gardener and Home Maker of Australia,* also strongly encouraged the use of native trees and shrubs. It published a series of Aboriginal stories about Australian plants, articles about gardens featuring native plants, and lists of native plants for the various seasons and for different uses.

Several descriptions of gardens in Sydney in *The Garden and the Home* magazine are evidence of the way native plants and exotics were mixed in gardens of the time. The journal described Lorne at Killara in its November 1923 issue, with its eucalypts and elk horns (*Platycerium bifercatum*) clinging to its trees. There were other native flora,

They line the drive and are set off by the lawns. Exotics are clearly established around the house. The geraniums (*Pelargonium* spp.) are from cuttings from

Amy Mack's description and photographs of the Australian garden started in the 1890s at Tregoyd overlooking Balmoral Beach on Sydney Harbour

Reproduced from *The Home,* December 1920

The Brownlow Hill
garden is one of
Australia's finest
examples of the
gardenesque style

Hardy Wilson, 1881–1955
Detail from *Entrance to
Brownlow Hill, Camden,
NSW*, 1919
pencil; 45.4 x 34.9 cm
From the Pictorial
Collection

yellow pea (*Epacris longiflora*), native ferns and the rock lily (*Dendrobium* spp.). It also had daisies, forget-me-nots, nerines and *Clivia nobilis*. There was a vegetable garden to one side and an orchard at the back. It had a celebrated rose garden with borders of violets.

Another remarkable garden to feature in *The Garden and the Home* magazine in 1923 was Frikfort at Marrickville in Sydney. It had roses all the way to the house and a hedge of pink roses and a giant Moreton Bay fig (*Ficus macrophylla*) with a host of stag horns (*Platycerium superbum*) hanging from it. It had a lawn under an English oak (*Quercus robur*), a rustic seat under an Irish strawberry tree (*Arbutus unedo*), a stately blueberry ash (*Elaeocarpus reticulatus*) and camellias, including the tea tree (*Camellia sinensis*). The reporter from the magazine observed that nature had run riot with:

> a beautiful medley of plants, a white bride
> rose beside a fleshy desert plant from Africa,
> a flat Japanese rose near an American
> chestnut, a fantastic cape strelitzia not far
> from a golden laburnum, northern and

Norfolk Island pines, a kauri pine (whether Australian or New Zealand is not clear), a silky oak (*Grevillea robusta*), the beautiful red-flowering Illawarra flame tree from just south of Sydney (*Brachychiton acerifolius*) and much else.

The Garden and the Home for January 1924 described another garden, Hervile at Killara, a suburb of Sydney, as having standard roses along a red gravel drive, under-planted with ground covers. It had many species of magnolias and maples, and the Australian bunya-bunya pine (*Araucaria bidwillii*). Also featured were: daphne, many jasmines and syringa, rhododendrons, azaleas and hydrangeas, the Australian climber *Hardenbergia violacea* and the exotic *Antignon* spp., bougainvillea and clematis.

Strathfield, the home of Joseph Vickery, another outstanding garden of the period, was described in *The Garden and the Home* for February 1924. It had eucalypts, camphor trees (*Cinnamomum camphora*), many prunus, jacarandas (*Jacaranda mimosifolia*), mandarins, olives, the bunya-bunya pine and silky

Country garden design
in the Walling style

Markdale, Binda,
New South Wales
Photograph by
Trisha Dixon

oaks. The serpentine gravelled drive was edged with turf and lined with Orleans roses. Behind them were poles for dahlias and chrysanthemums. There was a *Mina lobata* along the tennis-court fence covering a

hundred feet of fence and a wonga-wonga vine (*Pandora pandorana*). The spiky New Zealand flax (*Phormium tenax*), *Euphorbia splendens* and the sacred bamboo (*Nandina domestica*), bananas

60

(*Musa* spp.), *Dracaena* species, and *Agave americana* mingled with the Chinese fan palm (*Livistona chinensis*) and the Canary date palm (*Phoenix canariensis*). The Australian boronia, Christmas bush (*Ceratopetalum gummiferum*), the flame pea (*Chorizema* spp.), Geraldton wax (*Chamelaucium uncinatum*), Didiscus (*Trachymene coerulea*) and *Stenocarpus cunninghammii* indicate the range of Australian plants, many from across the continent, that were available to

gardeners in Sydney. Varieties of roses included Comptesse de Cayla, American pillar, climbing Orleans, Dorothy Perkins and Hiawatha. And there was much, much more. The reporter called this a natural garden!

These detailed descriptions show the extent to which Australian plants were appreciated well before the native garden movement of the later years of the twentieth century; and that they were planted in joyous riot with exotic plants from all over the world.

The history of gardening in Australia has not till recently been marked by many Australian garden designers of wide repute. Guilfoyle in the nineteenth century was one. Three others stand out in the early to mid-twentieth century: Edna Walling, Jocelyn Brown and Paul Sorensen.

Edna Walling was born in England and came to Australia with her family in 1912 when she was sixteen. She entered Burnley Agricultural College in Melbourne in 1916 and after graduating became a gardening labourer. Two years later she became inspired by 'a stone wall supporting a semi-circular terrace; I was fascinated … I shall build walls, I found myself solemnly registering'. She turned to design, creating formal designs for others while establishing a small garden and bushland around her own cottage. In the 1920s she bought a tract of land on the outskirts of Melbourne and created a village called Bickleigh Vale,

Edna Walling believed this garden to be her finest creation

Mawarra, Sherbrooke, Victoria
Photograph by Trisha Dixon

Entrance to an
Edna Walling
walled garden
Cruden Farm,
Langwarrin, Victoria
Photograph by
Trisha Dixon

where she lived for many years. Seventy years later the gardens still reflect her influence.

Walling melded the influence of Gertrude Jekyll and William Robinson, both English garden designers, with her own attraction for Australian native plants. Jekyll worked with the architect of New Delhi, Edwin Lutyens, designing gardens in the new tradition of the Arts and Crafts Movement. The strong architecture of Lutyens combined with the artistic and colourful plantings of Jekyll became their trademark. Jekyll was also influenced by Robinson, the writer of *The Wild Garden*, published in 1870 and the owner/editor of the English journal *The Garden* which extolled the beauty of English wildflowers and 'rustic' decoration in the garden. Robinson reacted against the gardenesque and Victorian stylised and exotic gardening. Interestingly, both Jekyll and Robinson are directly influencing today's gardeners

through the republication of their writings and their outspoken disciples.

Walling's work ranged from simple cottage gardens to more sophisticated gardens for large houses in the cities, in the hills outside the main cities, and on pastoral properties. A solid underlying framework, including her much-loved stone walls, terraces and steps, was softened by exuberant plantings.

She wrote regularly in the *Australian Home Beautiful* for twenty years, as well as writing five enormously successful books, one of which was published posthumously. Here she describes her particular love of the Australian landscape and native plants:

How pleasant a light is thrown upon the subject of making new gardens from a study of those we have been looking at in the mountains and other wild places. How important the topography is. How vital every boulder providing a sheltered pocket, or holding back some steep bank. There never seems to be any spare earth in these gardens of Nature's making.

Pergola for a large
country garden designed
by Edna Walling

The Wild Garden at
Boortkoi, Hexham, Victoria
Photograph by
Trisha Dixon

In 1967, as suburbia encroached on Bickleigh Vale, she moved to Buderim in Queensland, where she started another garden which was to reflect a change in her thinking. 'This garden of mine is not going to be a fashionable one of native plants, much as I love natives. My garden will be stuffed full of as many of the old-world flowers as I can find that will thrive happily in this rather humid climate.' Unfortunately, poor health prevented her from seeing this garden grow into maturity.

Jocelyn Brown, a Sydney garden designer, came into prominence in the 1930s and 1940s. She married an architect, Alfred Brown, and they spent time in England after the First World War, living in Welwyn Garden City where Alfred worked for the city architect. The Garden City Movement was influential on both of them as was the Arts and Crafts Movement. The legacy of Gertrude Jekyll shaped Jocelyn's judgement. She enjoyed mixing the symmetrical and the asymmetrical and over-planting for a lavish effect. Regrettably, many of her gardens have not survived but her work is gaining recognition again through books and articles written about her.

Paul Sorensen was born in Denmark in 1890. He arrived in Australia in 1915 after studying horticulture in Denmark and working for a Copenhagen nursery and at the Villa Hvidore, the summer home of the Queen of Denmark. The First World War and one of the worst droughts in recorded time meant there was little employment, especially for a gardener, so he went to work on a property as a general hand and grower of vegetables. The drought and the fierce dust led him to advise

Jocelyn Brown's
Sydney home
Greenwood, St Ives,
New South Wales
Photograph by
Trisha Dixon

65

A Paul Sorensen designed
garden

Bethune, West Guyong,
New South Wales
Photograph by Trisha Dixon

people later: 'In Australia don't buy land, buy water.' The experience gave him a chance to absorb some feeling for the Australian flora, and when he began designing, he did not ignore native plants. Instead he mixed his palette, choosing the plant appropriate for what he wanted it to do. The gardens he is most associated with are the larger gardens of the Blue Mountains and the Western Plains of New South Wales although he also designed a number of small, urban gardens.

Sorensen was influenced not by Robinson and Jekyll, but by a European interpretation of Capability Brown and Humphrey Repton through his own teachers and first employers in Copenhagen. He was interested in spaces and in large plants. Trees

Paul Sorensen's
landscape of sweeping
lawns and mature trees
Invergowrie, Exeter,
New South Wales
Photograph by
Trisha Dixon

were the most significant element in his design. In his gardens, the mature effects are the lovely contrast and melding of foliage of all types offset by wide lawns. His nursery in the Blue Mountains is planted with trees which make it more like a garden than the average nursery.

He died at Leura in the Blue Mountains in 1983, working till the end of his life. Unlike Edna Walling he did not write. His work is remembered through gardens like Everglades, Fjellheim II, Blue Mist and Cheppen and more recently through Richard Ratcliffe's writings and lectures.

The contributions of these three people—Walling, Brown and Sorensen—spanned the middle of the century, and the work of Walling and Sorensen continues to influence the gardens of today.

CHAPTER 6
An Evolution

The portable garden

Photograph by Trisha Dixon

Since the 1960s the range of Australian garden styles has continued to grow, influenced by the increasing mobility of Australians, the influx of migrants, television programs, films and the masses of gardening books and magazines.

A decorative interpretation of the English cottage garden, with an emphasis on English plants such as bluebells and hyacinths, night-scented stocks, old fashioned roses, pinks, iris and columbine, has become very fashionable. This fashion represents a romantic, idealised view of the original cottage garden because, in most cases, the latter's very practical and productive nature is overlooked. In the decorative English cottage garden of today any utilitarian aspects are usually concealed and there is not a strong emphasis on the production of food.

While Australian plants do not feature strongly in these gardens, there is a push by nurseries and some publications to include those Australian plants that lend themselves to the cottage garden design. Larger Australian plants which were already in the garden, like eucalypts, may be left to give an Australian flavour.

Another style of garden which is enjoying a resurgence is the larger, more formal garden, often described as an English garden. While it never disappeared, at least in the cooler, high-rainfall areas, such as Victoria and Tasmania and the tablelands and highlands of New South Wales, it has been particularly celebrated in recent times through the garden visiting movement. Most are recognisably Australian because of the borrowed landscapes of paddocks and the grey-green of the eucalypts, wattles and other native shrubs. While English

Creative use of a 'backyard'

Rose Cottage, Beechworth, Victoria
Photograph by
Trisha Dixon

gardens generally merge into the English landscape, there is a perceptible division between the garden and the landscape in the Australian version. This is not unattractive, but it is different; the grey-green colours together with the strong Australian light, even in winter, emphasise that difference.

Formal gardens are having a strong revival and topiary, or shaped plants, are once again in vogue. This may be a reaction to the denseness of some native gardens or the blowzy lushness of the cottage garden, or simply the result of television and book publishing influences.

The native garden movement that began in the 1890s exploded in the 1950s and 1960s and then suffered a decline in popularity in the 1980s as many gardens became overgrown, untidy and lanky. It was a fairly common, but uninformed, belief that the native garden was a trouble-free or low-maintenance garden. At that time, horticultural knowledge lagged behind the enthusiasm for all-native gardens which, in fact, needed careful tending and pruning. Some plants died out or became unhealthy in the artificial environment; trees described as small grew too large for suburban gardens as they enjoyed the

unaccustomed increase in water; and the larger plants gradually took over from the smaller ones. The ecologist Professor Nix observed that his own garden changed from a heath-like garden to a forest-like environment in only two decades.

The streetscapes of Aranda, a Canberra suburb built on the slopes of Black Mountain at the height of the native garden movement in the late 1950s and 1960s, reveal the triumphs and failures of the native garden. The best gardens are lovely backgrounds for

Suburban garden blending exotic and indigenous plants
Dimpel garden, Farrer, Australian Capital Territory
Photograph by Trisha Dixon

family life. Others demonstrate the problems of believing that native gardens are low-maintenance gardens.

In the 1990s there has been a change in native gardens. No longer purely native, they now include some exotics. The Dimpel garden, in the arid Canberra suburb of Farrer, is an example of this. While it was intended to contain only Australian plants, Mrs Dimpel's love of plants she knew in Germany has led to a successful blending of native and exotic. The front garden is almost entirely native and the side and back gardens have a mix. Mr Dimpel has 'borrowed' some of the tiny reserve at

Where once there were gardeners to keep some semblance of order, judicious neglect has resulted in a more relaxed style of country garden

Bobundara, Monaro, New South Wales
Photograph by Trisha Dixon

Percy F.S. Spence
Bobundara, an Early Australian Homestead

Reproduced from *Australia* (London: Adam and Charles Black, 1910)

one side and the Farrer Ridge reserve at the back to create a landscape which makes the surrounding suburb seem miles away. Lawns are used sparingly: they sweep up from the drive to make a path to the side of the house and set off a lovely group of eucalypts on a rise, a small pool near the dining room, and the flowery beds rising up the slope. Elsewhere the paths are mulched for walking.

Another native garden, in Melbourne, is a cross between two styles: it is a native garden but instead of a bush setting it has strong architectural lines and a formal structure. Low water use is a priority. Created by Chapman and Faulkner Landscape Design, the garden repeats the lines of the house and is designed to bring a view of the

Dandenongs into the garden. Native and exotic are successfully combined because they were chosen for their similar water requirements. The natives receive an equal amount of treatment and in fact some are shaped. The hardy *Westringia* spp. has, for example, been successfully clipped into topiary forms. This shrub, found from Tasmania to Queensland, with its grey-green colouring, its delicate white or pale violet coloured flowers which appear in winter, its hardiness against heat, cold and the salty blast of sea winds and

above
Trompe l'oeil effect creates understated elegance in the front entrance to a suburban home

Berger garden, Forrest, Australian Capital Territory
Photograph by Trisha Dixon

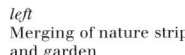

left
Merging of nature strip and garden

Maggie Shepherd garden, Red Hill, Australian Capital Territory
Photograph by Trisha Dixon

far left
Australian topiary: Westringia is clipped into a dense ball

Photograph courtesy of *Landscape Australia* magazine

Garden design adapted to harsh environment

Seddon garden, Fremantle, Western Australia

Photograph by Ralph Neale

its tolerance of pruning, has become one of the most versatile of Australian plants.

The battle against harsh conditions is continuous in many gardens and Professor George Seddon, landscape architect, philosopher and writer, has described how he and his wife cope with the difficult conditions of their fifth garden in Fremantle,

Western Australia. The garden is exposed to strong salt-laden winds coming off the Indian Ocean and is on a fine white calcareous sand which repels water and contains little organic matter. The rain falls mainly in winter with none at all from November to March when the heat dries out everything. His solution is drought-tolerant plants and paving. He could not develop a native garden to match his house and other buildings from last century because most Australian plants will not tolerate alkaline soils. Taking his own best advice, he prowled the nearby gardens to see what was growing. Mediterranean plants have been the answer, as they are in many gardens. Artemisia, lavender, oleander and oaks from the Mediterranean (Cork Oak, *Quercus suber*, the Italian Evergreen Oak, *Quercus ilex* and the Algerian Oak, *Quercus canariensis*). Professor Seddon struck cuttings from single-flowered oleanders from the local cemetery when he could not find the colours he wanted in nurseries. African plants have also found a place, particularly 'good old agapanthus'. The Swan River cypress (*Actinostrobus pyramidalis*) and *Bauhinia hookeri* with its crimson-edged

flowers are two Australian trees that thrive in this difficult environment.

The nature strip is a significant element in the modern streetscape and it is seen at its best in the national capital. Designed as a garden city, Canberra incorporates nature strips along many of its streets. Most consist of native or exotic trees with a plain lawn underneath in the American style. Increasingly,

Elegance of the white trunks of eucalypts along one of Canberra's most stately streets *(Eucalyptus mannifera* spp. *maculosa)*

Mugga Way, Red Hill, Australian Capital Territory
Photograph by Trisha Dixon

The illusion of country
in the city with the use
of natural landscape
elements such as
winding gravel drive,
towering eucalypts and
mass plantings of
agapanthus
Bickleigh Vale,
Mooroolbark, Victoria
Photograph by
Trisha Dixon

however, gardeners are decorating their nature strips with dense plantings of natives or exotics and incorporating the nature strip into the design of their front gardens. Other gardeners faced with extra grass to mow and water abandon the grass and plant low-maintenance creepers over the area.

Quite commonly in suburban gardens the drive has become the path to the house as well. This has caused a decline in that long-popular feature, the front garden divided symmetrically in two by a central path to the front door. Now the drive serves both purposes with a small path leading off it to the front door. The concrete driveway of the 1950s and 1960s is being replaced by attractive paving and elegant plantings. So too, the garage, with its dominating appearance, is being replaced by the carport. The Dimpel's drive is more like a wide path. It winds past the garages on the side of the house with central plantings to break up the expanse of turning circle, to the kitchen and a carport at the back. It is beautifully paved and rhododendrons, perennial phlox, *Lomandra longifolia* and many other plants tumble over the edges. The carport is a place for shade in summer and hanging baskets are filled with more tender plants.

far left
**Five Virtues Courtyard
Garden designed by
Paul Sheppard**

Melbourne, Victoria
Photograph courtesy of
Landscape Australia
magazine

left
**The sense of enclosure
is a strong element in
garden design**

Hanaminno, Boorowa,
New South Wales
Photograph by
Trisha Dixon

Though the quarter acre block endures, the trend, particularly in the inner suburbs, is toward medium-density living, creating a series of new challenges for Australian gardeners. One consequence has been the popularity of the courtyard garden. Paul Sheppard's design for a cluster of townhouses in Melbourne provides an outstanding example of the Japanese influence. The Xanthorrhoea Garden is the entrance courtyard of one of the houses. It has a very limited number of

Informal planting
surrounds an
expanse of water in
a country garden
**Longfield, Robertson,
New South Wales
Photograph by
Trisha Dixon**

plants with a grass tree (*Xanthorrhoea australis*) facing the entrance gate. The Bamboo Screen Courtyard has screens supporting climbers such as clematis and the verandahs are of bamboo. The Five Virtues Courtyard Garden, the five Confucian

virtues, is a more densely planted garden. The Teahouse Style Garden is a sparsely planted garden, designed to show the serenity of plants and space.

An atrium of a house in Melbourne, designed by Ivan Stranger, has classical references but it is entirely modern in its planting. The enclosure and light from a glass roof allows a tropical garden to grow in a cool climate. The lushness and the sound of the waterfall soothe the senses. Plants are a mix of native and exotic such as *Spathiphyllum phryniifolium*, *Dracaena marginata* and *Archontophoenix cunninghamiana,* the Bangalow palm. Baby's tears (*Helxine solierolii*) is planted along the stream.

In a space of half an acre, Polly Park has designed a remarkable garden in Canberra. She has created a classic American front garden, a classical Italian parterre, a knot garden, an Indian garden, a modern classical garden inspired by the Brazilian designer

left and above
Broad-leafed plants provide the middle level of the canopy and palms provide the upper storey in an atrium designed by Ivan Stranger

Toorak, Victoria
Photographs courtesy of *Landscape Australia* magazine

Burle Marx, as well as other gardens. Each of these is complete and in a 'room' of its own, except for the miniature garden and knot garden. Many visitors come to this garden: some study it, others meditate in the Japanese garden, but all enjoy it.

The idiosyncratic garden has probably been with us since gardening began. Producing something other than the plant garden is a labour of love for some people who also produce the most amazing effects to stun passers-by. The reasons they are made are as various as people's interests. In Griffith, a

suburb of Canberra, there is a garden commemorating the people of Oradour sur Glane in France who were massacred in the Second World War. It has been made by an RAF rear gunner who, after being shot down, was looked after by the people of this village. The garden is a garden of memories, telling the story to those who might otherwise not hear it.

Italian-style parterre with
meticulously trained ivy ornamenting
the brush fences enclosing the garden

Boxford, Red Hill,
Australian Capital Territory
Photograph by Trisha Dixon

The horse trough in this contemporary country garden is one of many visual metaphors used by landscape architect Vladimir Sitta

Garangula, Harden, New South Wales Photograph by Trisha Dixon

At Garangula in Harden, New South Wales, Vladimir Sitta has designed a modernistic masterpiece. Once a traditional farm garden around a nineteenth-century house, it has been transformed into a work of art. Sitta has used the land like a piece of canvas, shaping the earth and using aesthetic and atmospheric elements such as a water trough, a sunken green cathedral and water mist.

Garangula is functional and aesthetic. It has purely modern elements, but with references to traditions and classical styles of the past. Like so many Australian gardens, it features an unselfconscious mix of native and exotic plants. And like so many others, it is the product of a tradition that began when convicts planted the first seeds of a vegetable plot just three days after their arrival; a tradition that has seen Australian gardeners blend overseas ideas, plants and styles with the bush flora and the climate that so confounded them in the early years of settlement. For more than two centuries that tradition has been producing an eclecticism that is reflected at once in so many styles and mixes of styles and yet in just one style: the Australian gardening style. An evolving style that produces Australia's timeless gardens.

An Evolution

81

A country lane
Langley Vale, Kyneton, Victoria
Photograph by Trisha Dixon

The following articles and books have been directly consulted in the preparation of this work.

Blainey, Geoffrey, *The Tyranny of Distance*. South Melbourne: Macmillan, 1974.

Bligh, Beatrice, *Cherish the Earth: the Story of Gardening in Australia*. Sydney: Ure Smith in association with the National Trust of Australia (NSW), 1973.

Brown, Jane, *Gardens of a Golden Afternoon: the Story of a Partnership: Edwin Lutyens and Getrude Jekyll*. London: Allen Lane, 1982.

Bunce, Daniel, *1836 Catalogue of Seeds and Plants*. Canberra: Mulini Press, 1994. Facsimile reprint of original.

Carter, Harold B., *Sir Joseph Banks, 1743–1820*. London: British Museum, 1988.

Crittenden, Victor, *A Shrub in the Landscape of Fame: Thomas Shepherd Australian Landscape Gardener and Nurseryman*. Canberra: Mulini Press, 1992.

—*The Front Garden: the Story of the Cottage Garden in Australia*. Canberra: Mulini Press, 1979.

Dixon, Trisha and Churchill, Jennie, *Gardens in Time: in the Footsteps of Edna Walling*. North Ryde, NSW: Angus & Robertson, 1988.

Fairbrother, Nan, *Men and Gardens*. London: Hogarth Press, 1956.

Harris, David R., 'Subsistence Strategies across Torres Strait', *Sunda and Sahul: Prehistoric Studies in Southeast Asia, Melanesia and Australia* (ed. by J. Allen, J. Golson and R. Jones). London: Academic Press, 1977.

Irving, Robert (comp.), *The History and Design of the Australian House*. Melbourne: Oxford University Press, 1985.

Knopwood, Robert, *Bobby Knopwood and His Times* edited by Mabel Hookey. Hobart: Fuller, 1929.

Lockley, J.G., *Rose-growing Made Easy*. Sydney: Cornstalk Publishing Company, 1927.

Lord, Ernest E., *Shrubs and Trees for Australian Gardens*. Melbourne: Lothian, 1982.

Lycett, Joseph, *Views in Australia, cr New South Wales and Van Diemen's Land Delineated ... .* London: J. Souter, c.1824.

Mitchell, Sir Thomas, *Three Expeditions into the Interior of Eastern Australia ... .* London: T. & W. Boone, 1838.

Pescott, R.T.M., *The Royal Botanic Gardens, Melbourne: a History from 1845–1970*. Melbourne: Oxford University Press, 1982.

Ratcliffe, Richard, *Australia's Master Gardener: Paul Sorensen and his Gardens*. Kenthurst, NSW: Kangaroo Press, 1990.

Royal Horticultural Society, *Gardener's Encyclopaedia of Plants and Flowers*. London: Royal Horticultural Society, 1989.

Seddon, George, 'The Evolution of a Gardener', *Landscape Australia*, 4/1995–1/1996.

Simons, Phyl Frazer, *Historic Tasmanian Gardens*. Canberra: Mulini Press, 1987.

Simpfendorfer, K.J., *An Introduction to Trees for South Eastern Australia*. Melbourne: Inkata Press, 1975.

Tench, Watkin, *A Complete Account of the Settlement at Port Jackson, in New South Wales ... *. London: G. Nicol, 1793.

—*A Narrative of the Expedition to Botany Bay ... *. London: J. Debrett, 1789.

Upitis, Astrida (ed.), *Durham Hall Garden near Braidwood New South Wales*. Canberra: Australian Garden History Society, ACT, Monaro and Riverina Branch, 1992.

Walling, Edna, *On the Trail of Australian Wildflowers*. Canberra: Mulini Press, 1984.

Wallis, James, *An Historical Account of the Colony of New South Wales and its Dependent Settlements ... *. London: R. Ackermann, 1821.

Wrigley, John W., *Australian Native Plants: a Manual for their Propogation, Cultivation and Use in Landscaping*. Sydney: Collins, 1988.

Borrowed landscape

Using the surrounding landscape as a design tool by leaving vistas from the garden to the countryside beyond.

Federation garden

A product of the 1890s to 1920s, complementing the Federation-style house with its boldly decorative details. Assymetrical in design, the garden was usually simple in style to offset and frame the ornate house. Paths and driveways were often curved to give an informal effect with areas of well-kept lawn and a minimum of garden beds.

Gardenesque style

A style of garden first used by J.C. Loudon in 1832 to describe a type of planting in which each individual plant was allowed to develop its natural character. The term was subsequently used to describe a style of garden layout characterised by winding paths, botanic interest, subtle use of urns and arches, and flowers.

Grotto

A natural or contrived cave used as a cool retreat in a garden, often adorned with stones, shells and used for growing ferns and shade-loving plants.

Ha-ha

A sunken fence or retaining wall that is not seen from within the garden, giving the impression of the garden carrying through into the landscape.

Landscape style

A revolutionary departure from the formal garden style with its regimented axial planting. Its origins were in the late seventeenth century and at its height all flower beds and 'garden' objects were removed and the 'pure' landscape swept right up to the house.

Parterre

A decorative garden, usually designed on level ground in a symmetrical pattern, using clipped hedging, paths and shaped plants.

Picturesque style

A style based on the precept that landscape design should be picturesque, as in a perfectly composed painting. This presented a romanticised view of the landscape.

Topiary

The art of shaping plants into ornamental shapes. This practice has come in and out of fashion throughout the ages and is once again in vogue, particularly in city gardens.

Aborigines 4–5, 57
Angas, George French 28
Aranda, ACT 69
Artists 10, 28, 33, 38, 47
Artists' perceptions 10, 12–13

Backyards 70
Balfe, J. 45
Banks, Sir Joseph 2, 4–5
Berger garden, ACT 71
Bethune, NSW 65
Bibbenluke Inn, NSW 47
Bickleigh Vale, Vic. 49, 61–2, 74
Bilgoela, NSW 56–7
Binnum Binnum, SA 32–4
Birchfield, NSW 39
Bligh, Governor William 9
Blue Mountains, NSW 66
Bobundara, NSW 70
Boortkoi, Vic. 63
Borrowed landscapes 11, 68, 70–1, 84
Botany Bay 4
Bowes Smyth, Arthur—see Smyth, Arthur Bowes
Boxford, ACT 77–9
Bradley, William 6
Braidwood, NSW 29–31
Brown, Jocelyn 61, 64, 66
Brown, Lancelot 'Capability' 66
Brownlow Hill, NSW 58
Bruce, Robert 6
Buddabuddah, NSW 45, 47
Buderim, Qld 64
Buninyong, Vic. 31
Burwood Villa, NSW 14
Bush 10, 61–2
Bush houses 43

Caire, Nicholas 41
Campbell, Robert 10
Campbell, Sophia 16–17
Cannan, Jane Dorothea 23
Cape of Good Hope 5
Cape Town 2
Carmichael, John 2

Cazneaux, Harold 55–6
Challicum, Vic. 21–3
Chapman and Faulkner Landscape Design 71
Clark, John Heaviside 7
Climate 5, 14, 16
Cogné, Francis 31
Cook, Captain James 2, 4, 17
Coombe Cottage, Vic. 52
Coonong, NSW 44–5
Cooper, Duncan 21–2
Courtyards 55–6, 75, 77
Cox River, NSW 43
Craig End, NSW 26
Crittenden, Victor 17
Cruden Farm, Vic. 62

Dayes, Edward 6
Derriweit, Vic. 38
Dimpel garden, ACT 69–71, 74
Dixon, Trisha 1, 15, 25, 30–1, 35–6, 39, 41, 47, 48, 49, 60–71, 73–6, 78–81
Drives 10, 51, 74
Drought 6
Durham Hall, NSW 29–31

Earle, Augustus iv
East Indies 4
E.T. (artist) 23
Everglades, NSW 66
Eyre, John 7, 10

Fences 9–10, 12–14, 23, 43, 47
First Fleet 2, 6, 28, 57, 80
Forest clearing 14
Fowkes, Francis 2–3
Frikfort, NSW 59
Furneaux, Tobias 17

Garangula, NSW 41, 80
Garden cities 17, 64
Garden designers 9, 35–6, 61–6
Garden styles
    American 55, 77

Classical—see Garden styles, Formal
Contemporary 77, 80
Cottage 10, 16, 20, 23, 29, 35, 40–1, 62, 68
Eclectic 29, 80
Federation 50, 84
Formal 9, 29, 34–5, 52–3, 68–9, 77, 79
Gardenesque 18–20, 27, 29, 34, 51–8, 84
Geometric 8–10, 12, 14, 21, 51
Idiosyncratic 78
Influences on 29
Japanese 75, 78
Landscape 9, 35–8, 84
Picturesque 9, 10, 11–14, 18, 84
Victorian 30–1
Gardeners 5, 26, 45
Gardeners, Chinese 41, 48
Gardens, ACT 69–71, 73, 74, 77–79
Gardens, botanical
    Melbourne 36, 38
    Sydney 14
    Tasmania 20
Gardens, democracy of 16–17
Gardens, English 16, 20, 27, 68
Gardens, Indian 77
Gardens, kitchen—see Gardens, productive
Gardens, knot 77
Gardens, native 55–6, 69–70
Gardens, native and exotic 55–61, 70–1
Gardens, NSW 2–14, 23–4, 26, 28–30, 34–5, 37, 39, 41, 43, 45, 47, 53–60, 64–6, 70, 75, 76
Gardens, productive 6, 10, 12–13, 39, 40–8, 45, 47–8, 55, 59
Gardens, Qld 64
Gardens, Roman 53
Gardens, Tas. 15, 17–19, 35, 46–7
Gardens, vegetable—see Gardens, productive

Gardens, Vic. 21, 28, 31, 35–6, 41, 48, 49, 52, 61–3, 68, 71, 74, 75, 77, 81
Gardens, walled 62
Gardens, WA 20–1, 27, 72–3
Gill, S.T. 29
Glass, James 28
Gondwana iv, 25, 27
Government House, first garden 2, 6–8, 14
Graham, Harold J. 46–7
Griffin, Walter Burley 57
Guerard, Eugene von 28–9
Guilfoyle, William 35–8

Ha-ha 21, 84
Hanaminno, NSW 75
Hedges 31, 52, 55
Hervile, NSW 59
Highfield, Tas. 18–19
Himely, Sigismond 11
Hobart, Tas. 17
Horticultural societies 29
Hose 50

India 6, 21, 27–8
Invergowrie, NSW 66

Jekyll, Gertrude 62, 64, 66
Jobson, Frederick 34

Kerry, Charles 35, 42
King George Sound, WA 27
Knopwood, Rev. Robert 17

Landscape Australia 71, 75, 77
Langley Vale, Vic. 81
Lawn-mower 26, 50
Lawns 7, 9, 36, 41, 51, 71
Leighton, Stanley 32–3
Lewin, John W. 8–10
Longfield, NSW 76
Lord Howe Island 5
Lorne, NSW 57, 59
Loudon, John Claudius 20, 84
Lutyens, Sir Edwin 62

INDEX

Lycett, Joseph 13–14, 18

McArthur garden 34
McCaughey, Sir Samuel 44–5
Mack, Amy 55–7
Markdale, NSW 60
Marx, Burle 78
Mawarra, Vic. 61
Melba, Dame Nellie 52
Mitchell, Sir Thomas 24
Moore, John D. 50–1
Moredun, NSW 23
Mort, T.S. 28
Mueller, Baron Ferdinand von 36

Nature strips 73–4
New England, NSW 23
New Guinea 27
New South Wales
    Early settlement 2–14
New Zealand 17, 27
Newcastle, NSW 16–17
Newington, NSW 54
Nix, Professor Henry 69
Norfolk Island 6
Nurseries 14, 20, 66, 68

Oradour sur Glane, France 78
Orchards 14, 18, 55, 59

Park, Polly 77–9
Parramatta, NSW 13–14
Parterre 77, 79, 84
Paths 51
Peacock, G.E. 26
Pergolas 52, 63
Phillip, Governor Arthur 4–5, 16
Photographers 35, 41
Piper, Captain John 13
Port Jackson—see Sydney
Preston, W. 10

Quarter acre block 16, 75

Ratcliffe, Richard 18, 66
Rees, Lloyd 51

Repton, Humphrey 66
Reveley, Henry W. 20–1
Riley, Alexander 14
Rio de Janeiro 2, 5
Robinson, William 62, 66
Rose Cottage, Vic. 68
Rose Hill—see Parramatta
Roseneath Ferry, Tas. 18
Rossi, Captain 24
Rossiville, NSW 24, 37
Rowan, Ellis 38
Royd, O. & D. 30
Rupertswood, Vic. 34

Scott, Pam 47
Seddon, George 72–3
Shepherd, Maggie 71
Shepherd, Thomas 14
Sheppard, Paul 75, 77
Sitta, Vladimir, 80
Smyth, Surgeon Arthur Bowes
    6, 57
Soil 5, 16
Sorensen, Paul 61, 64–6
Spence, Percy F.S. 70
Spring Vale, Tas. 15
Stonework 49, 61–2
Stranger, Ivan 77
Strathfield, NSW 59
Sydney 2–14

Taylor, Major James 10, 12
Tench, Captain Watkin 4–5, 12
Tennis courts 55, 60
Topiary 69, 71, 84
Tregoyd, NSW 56–7

Ultimo, NSW 10

Verandahs 23, 55
Vickery, Joseph 59

Walling, Edna 49, 60–4, 66
Wallis, Captain James 10
Warre, Henry James 27
Weston, Charles 57

Wilson, William Hardy 35, 52–4,
    58
Woolloomooloo, NSW 10–12
Woolongoon, Vic. 48

Yandilla Station, Qld 29

INDEX OF PLANT NAMES

Common names for groups of plants are used where it is not clear which genus is referred to. Individual varieties of roses are listed under *Rosa* spp.

Acacia spp. 20, 52, 68
    A. longifolia 28
    A. mearnsii viii
Acer spp. 59
Actinostrobus pyramidalis 72
Agapanthus spp. 72–4
Agathis spp. 59
Agave spp. 38
    A. americana 60
    A. stricta 27
Algerian Oak—*see Quercus canariensis*
American chestnut—*see Castanea* spp.
Annuals 52
Antignon spp. 59
Apium prostratum 4
Apple—*see Malus* spp.
Apricots—*see Prunus mume*
Aquilegia spp. 68
Araucaria spp.
    A. bidwillii 59
    A. heterophylla 4, 6, 8–9, 59
Arbutus unedo 59
Archontophoenix cunninghamiana 77
Artemisia spp. 72
Artichoke—*see Cynara scolymus*
Artocarpus altilis 5
Atlas cedar—*see Cedrus libani* ssp. *atlantica*
Atriplex spp. 35
Azalea—*see Rhododendron* spp.

Baby's tears—*see Helxine solierolii*

INDEX

Bamboo 23, 77
Bananas—*see Musa* spp.
Bangalow palm—*see
    Archontophoenix
    cunninghamiana*
*Bauhinia hookeri—see
    Livistona hookeri*
Birch—*see Betula* spp.
Bird of paradise flower—*see
    Strelitzia reginae*
Bitou bush—*see
    Chrysanthemoides monilifera*
Black wattle—*see Acacia
    mearnsii* and *Callicoma
    serratifolia*
Blue gum—*see Eucalyptus
    saligna*
Bluebell—*see Hyacinthoides* spp.
Blueberry ash—*see
    Elaeocarpus reticulatus*
Boronia spp. 61
Bougainvillea spp. 59
Box—*see Buxus* spp.
Brachychiton acerifolius 59
Briar—*see Rosa canina*
Bread fruit—*see Artocarpus
    altilis*
Brittle gum—*see Eucalyptus
    mannifera* ssp. *maculosa*
Bull Bay—*see Magnolia
    grandiflora*
Bunya-bunya pine—*see
    Araucaria bidwillii*
Buxus spp. 30–1, 78

Cabbage tree—*see Cordyline*
spp.
Cabbage tree palms—*see
    Livistona australis*
Cacti 27
Callicoma serratifolia viii
Callitris preissii
Camellia spp. 59
    C. sinensis 59
Camphor trees—*see
    Cinnamomum camphora*

Canary date palm/Canary
    Islands Palm—*see Phoenix
    canariensis*
Castanea spp. 59
Casuarina spp. 14, 20
Cedar—*see Cedrus* spp.
Cedrus spp. 31
    C. libani ssp. *atlantica* 31
Century plant—*see Agave
    americana*
Ceratopetalum gummiferum 61
Chamelaucium uncinatum 61
Chestnut, American—*see
    Castanea* spp.
Chinese fan palm—*see
    Livistona chinensis*
Chorizema spp. 61
Christmas bush—*see
    Ceratopetalum gummiferum*
Chrysanthemum spp. 59
Chrysanthemoides monilifera 28
Cinnamomum camphora 59
Citrus spp.
    C. aurantifolia 52
    C. limon 52
    C. reticulata 52, 59
    C. sinensis 5, 14, 52
Clematis spp. 59, 77
Climbers 23, 35, 43
Clivia nobilis 59
Conifers 18
Cordyline spp. 38
Cork oak—*see Quercus suber*
Crataegus spp. 31
Cupressus spp. 52, 54–5
    C. funebris 31
Cycad—*see Cycas media*
Cycas media 5
Cynara scolymus 45
Cypress—*see Cupressus* spp.

Dahlia spp. 59
Daisies 42, 59
Dandelion—*see Taraxacum* spp.
Daphne odora 59
Dendrobium spp. 59

Desmodium amethystinum 32
Dianthus spp. 68
*Didiscus caeruleus—see
    Trachymene coerulea*
Dioscorea spp. 5
    D. sativa var. *elongata* 5
Dracaena spp. 60
    D. marginata 77

Elaeocarpus reticulatus 59
Elk horn—*see Platycerium
    bifercatum*
Elm—*see Ulmus* spp.
English oak—*see Quercus
    robur*
Epacris longiflora 57, 59
Eucalyptus spp. 12, 14, 20, 21,
    23, 28, 34–5, 43, 57, 59,68, 71,
    74
    E. ficifolia 38
    E. mannifera ssp. *maculosa* 73
    E. saligna 51
Euphorbia splendens 60

Ficus macrophylla 5, 59
Fig—*see Ficus* spp.
Ferns 59
Flame pea—*see Chorizema* spp.
Flowering gum—*see Eucalyptus
    ficifolia*
Forget-me-not—*see Myosotis*
    spp.

Geraldton wax—*see
    Chamelaucium uncinatum*
Geranium—*see Pelargonium*
    spp.
Globe artichoke—*see Cynara
    scolymus*
Golden chain tree—*see
    Laburnum* spp.
Grape—*see Vitus vinifera*
Grass 9, 17, 26, 34, 52
Grass tree—*see Xanthorrhoea
    australis*
Grevillea robusta 59

Hakea spp. 20
Hardenbergia violacea 59
Hawthorn—*see Crataegus* spp.
Hebe buxifolia
Helianthus spp. 42
Helxine solierolii 77
Holm oak—*see Quercus ilex*
Hoop pine—*see Araucaria
    cunninghamii*
Hyacinthoides spp. 68
Hydrangea spp. 51–3, 59

Illawarra flame tree—*see
    Brachychiton acerifolius*
Iris spp. 58, 68
Irish strawberry tree—*see
    Arbutus unedo*
Italian Evergreen Oak—*see
    Quercus ilex*

Jacaranda mimosifolia 38, 51–2,
    59
Jasmine—*see Jasminum* spp.
Jasminum spp. 59

Ka-aatha—*see Dioscorea* spp.
Kauri pine—*see Agathis* spp.
King protea—*see Protea
    cynaroides*

Laburnum spp. 59
Lavandula spp. 72
Lavatera assurgentiflora 21
Lavender—*see Lavandula* spp.
Lemon—*see Citrus limon*
Leptomeria acida 4
Ligustrum spp. 52
Lilac—*see Syringa* spp.
Lilies—*see Lilium* spp.
Lilium spp. 42
Lime—*see Citrus aurantifolia*
Livistona spp.
    L. australis 56
    L. hookeri 72
    L. chinensis 60
Lomandra longifolia 74

Lombardy poplar—*see Populus nigra* 'Italica'

Maclura pomifera 31–2
Magnolia spp. 59
  M. grandiflora 38
Malus spp. 5, 17
Mandarin—*see Citrus reticulata*
Maple—*see Acer* spp.
Mathiola spp. 68
Melia azedarach ssp. *australasica* 35
Melons 47
Mina lobata 59
Moreton Bay fig—*see Ficus macrophylla*
Musa spp. 60
Myosotis spp. 59

Nandina domestica 60
Native currant—*see Leptomeria acida*
Native fuchsia, native heath—*see Epacris longiflora*
Nectarine—*see Prunus persica* var. *nectarina*
Nerine bowdenii 59
Nerium spp. 35, 72
Nettles—*see Urtica dioica*
New Zealand flax—*see Phormium tenax*
New Zealand spinach—*see Tetragonia tetragonoides*
Norfolk Island pine—*see Araucaria heterophylla*
Northern pine—*see Pinus* spp.

Oaks—*see Quercus* spp.
Olea spp. 59
Oleander—*see Nerium* spp.
Olive—*see Olea* spp.
Opuntia spp. 28
Orange—*see Citrus sinensis*
Osage orange—*see Maclura pomifera*

Palm, Canary Island—*see Phoenix canariensis*
Palms 54–5, 77
Pandora pandorana 60
Pea, yellow—*see Epacris longiflora*
Peach—*see Prunus persica*
Pelargonium spp. 6, 57
Perennials 43
Phlox spp. 74
Phoenix canariensis 38, 61
Phormium tenax 4, 60
Pinks—*see Dianthus* spp.
Pinus spp. 59
Platycerium bifercatum 57
Platycerium superbum 59
Populus nigra var. 'Italica' 31
Prickly pear—*see Opuntia* spp.
Privet—*see Ligustrum* spp.
Protea spp. 27
  P. cynaroides iv, 25, 27
Prunus spp. 59
  P. mume 14
  P. persica 14
  P. persica var. *nectarina* 14

Quercus spp. 72
  Q. canariensis 72
  Q. ilex 72
  Q. robur 59
  Q. suber 72

Red flowering gum—*see Eucalyptus ficifolia*
Rhododendron spp. 38, 59, 74
Rock lily—*see Dendrobium* spp.
Rosa spp. 18, 29, 31–2, 43, 52, 59, 61, 68
  American pillar 61
  Bush tea 52
  Comptesse de Cayla 61
  Dorothy Perkins 61
  Hiawatha 61
  Japanese 59
  Maman Cochet 52
  Orleans 59, 61

Radiance 52
Safrano 52
White bride 59
  R. Canina 28
Rose—*see Rosa* spp.

Sacred bamboo—*see Nandina domestica*
Salix spp. 34
Salt bush—*see Atriplex* spp.
Sea celery—*see Apium prostratum*
Shrubs 7, 9, 17, 18, 22, 23, 28, 68
Silky oak—*see Grevillea robusta*
Spathiphyllum phryniifolium 77
Spider lily—*see Nerine* spp.
Stag horn—*see Platycerium superbum*
Stenocarpus cunninghammii 61
Stock—*see Mathiola* spp.
Strelitzia reginae 27, 59
Succulents 27
Sunflowers—*see Helianthus* spp.
Swamp cypress—*see Actinostrobus pyramidalis*
Swan River cypress—*see Callitris preissii*
Sydney blue gum—*see Eucalyptus saligna*
Syringa spp. 59

Taraxacum spp. 40
Tea tree—*see Camellia sinensis*
Telopea speciosissima 27
Tetragonia tetragonoides 4
Thampu—*see Dioscorea sativa* var. *elongata*
Trachymene coerulea 61
Tree mallow—*see Lavatera assurgentiflora*
Trees, fruit 5–6, 14, 43, 45, 47

Ulmus spp. 31

Urtica aioica 40

Vegetables 5–6, 17, 21, 40–4, 47,
Vines—*see Vitus vinifera*
Viola spp. 59
Violets—*see Viola* spp.
Vitus vinifera 5–6, 8, 12, 18, 21, 43, 45

Waratah—*see Telopea speciosissima*
Wattles—*see Acacia* spp.
Western Australian flowering gum—*see Eucalyptus ficifolia*
Westringia spp. 71
White cedar—*see Melia azedarach* spp. *australasica*
Wisteria sinensis 31
Wonga-wonga vine—*see Pandora pandorana*
Wormwood—*see Artemisia* spp.

Xanthorrhoea australis 1, 75–7

Yams—*see Dioscorea* spp.
Yucca spp. 33